Americans to the Moon

The Story of Project Apollo

July 20, 1969: Neil Armstrong and Buzz Aldrin walk on the surface of the moon. For the first time in history, man sets foot upon a celestial body that is not the earth. . . .

How was this great feat accomplished? When President John F. Kennedy in 1961 announced a national goal of landing men on the moon before 1970, no American had yet orbited the earth. Yet, within less than nine years, Project Apollo achieved the goal—with a technical precision that astounded hundreds of millions of viewers and listeners around the earth.

Gene Gurney described the earlier achievements of the national manned-space program in his books, *Americans Into Orbit: The Story of Project Mercury* and *Walk in Space: The Story of Project Gemini.* Now, in *Americans to the Moon,* Colonel Gurney continues with the even more spectacular achievements of Project Apollo.

Apollo 12 astronaut raises U.S. flag.

Americans
to the Moon

The Story of Project Apollo

by Gene Gurney

Illustrated with photographs

RANDOM HOUSE · NEW YORK

The Apollo Missions

APOLLO 1—Saturn 1B launched unmanned Apollo capsule on suborbital flight. First flight for rocket as well as capsule.

February 26, 1966

APOLLO 2—Saturn 1B launched unmanned Apollo capsule on suborbital flight to test capsule's ability to withstand high re-entry temperatures.

August 25, 1966

Planned as first manned Apollo flight; intended to orbit earth. During test on January 27, 1967, flash fire in capsule killed Astronauts Virgil I. Grissom, Edward H. White II, and Roger B. Chaffee.

Scheduled for February 1967

APOLLO 4—Saturn 5 launched unmanned capsule into earth orbit; first flight for giant new rocket. After two orbits capsule traveled 11,234 miles from earth.

November 9, 1967

APOLLO 5—Saturn 1B carried unmanned lunar landing module into earth orbit. First test in space of LM.

January 22, 1968

APOLLO 6—Further test of Saturn 5 and unmanned Apollo capsule. Capsule traveled 13,821 miles from earth.

April 4, 1968

APOLLO 7—Astronauts Walter M. Schirra, Donn F. Eisele, and Walter Cunningham made first manned Apollo flight. During 163 orbits of earth, they practiced simulated docking maneuvers. First TV presentation from American astronauts in space.

October 11, 1968

APOLLO 8—First manned flight to vicinity of moon. Astronauts Frank Borman, James A. Lovell, and William A. Anders made ten orbits of moon before returning to earth.

December 21, 1968

APOLLO 9—First manning in space of LM. Astronauts James McDivitt, David Scott, and Russell Schweickart flew Apollo capsule and LM in earth orbit.

March 3, 1969

APOLLO 10—Astronauts Thomas P. Stafford, John W. Young, and Eugene A. Cernan flew Apollo capsule and LM in lunar orbit. LM flew to within 9.4 miles of moon's surface, inspected possible landing area, and tested landing radar.

May 18, 1969

APOLLO 11—Astronauts Neil A. Armstrong, Edwin A. Aldrin, and Michael Collins flew capsule and LM in lunar orbit. LM made first manned landing on moon.

July 16, 1969

APOLLO 12—Astronauts Charles Conrad, Richard F. Gordon, and Alan L. Bean flew second lunar landing mission. Following precise landing close to Surveyor 3, Conrad and Bean conducted several experiments on lunar surface.

November 14, 1969

Contents

First Journey to the Moon

"We've got it! We've got it! Apollo 8 is in lunar orbit!"

The excited cry shattered the tense stillness in the Mission Control Center at the National Aeronautics and Space Administration's Manned Spacecraft Center in Houston, Texas. A cheer went up from the men seated at the consoles in Mission Control. For 36 long minutes they had received no information from Apollo 8. Now they knew that the three astronauts in the Apollo 8 spacecraft had safely begun the first of 10 trips around the moon. It was a truly epochal moment in the history of mankind.

Who were the brave men who were going to orbit the moon? And how had they managed to travel so far from the earth?

For the trail-blazing first journey to the moon, the National Aeronautics and Space Administration (NASA) had selected three of its astronauts—Air Force Colonel Frank Borman and Navy Captain James A. Lovell, Jr., both veterans of space travel, and Air Force Major William A. Anders, a space rookie. Their big adventure began at 2:36 A.M. on December 21, 1968. (All times given in this book are Eastern Standard Time.)

A tense moment in the Mission Control Center, Houston.

Dressed in pressure suits and carrying portable life-support systems, the Apollo 8 astronauts walk to the van which will take them to Launch Pad 39A. Front to back: Frank Borman, James Lovell, and William Anders.

They were awakened in the crew quarters of the Manned Spacecraft Operations building at NASA's John F. Kennedy Space Center, a rocket launching complex on Florida's east coast. The three astronauts had a final physical checkup and a breakfast of orange juice, steak, scrambled eggs, and toast before donning gleaming white spacesuits and large bubble helmets. Then, with Frank Borman leading the way, they boarded a white van for the six-mile ride to their spaceship.

It was still dark when the astronauts reached Launch Pad 39A, but bright floodlights illuminated the 282-foot-tall Saturn 5 booster that was going to carry them into space. Before entering a high-speed elevator for the ride up to their spacecraft, the three men paused to look at the vapor that swirled around the sides of the most powerful rocket men had ever flown. So far the countdown was right on schedule. Unless an unexpected problem developed, in three hours the Saturn 5 would lift them from

Pad 39A and they would be heading for the moon, 230,000 miles away.

At 7:51, exactly as planned, the Saturn thundered from Pad 39A, leaving behind a pool of flame and a towering cloud of smoke. "Loud and clear!" radioed Spacecraft Commander Frank Borman from Apollo 8 as the rocket roared into the sky followed by a 600-foot tail of flame.

"All looks great," replied Astronaut Michael Collins at Mission Control in Houston where he was handling voice communications with the spacecraft.

The Saturn 5 has three stages, or sections. The five engines of the first stage lift the rocket from the launching pad. After a few minutes of flight the first stage shuts down and falls away. The five smaller engines of the second stage take over, to be replaced in turn by the single engine of the third stage.

Three minutes after lift-off Borman radioed: "Staging was smooth." He was reporting that the Saturn's first stage had shut down and fallen away. "The ride now is even smoother," he added. Six minutes later the third stage replaced the second stage. It pushed Apollo 8 into an earth orbit before shutting down. Unlike the first and second stages, the third stage remained attached to the Apollo spacecraft. Its powerful engine would be needed again.

During the climb into orbit, the three astronauts had been strapped to their reclining couches. From the couches they watched the red, green, and amber lighted dials and displays on the spacecraft's instrument panel. They manipulated switches and controls as the need arose and between tasks they enjoyed

The Apollo 8 space vehicle, rocketing up from Launch Pad 39A, startles an egret.

the view from the spacecraft windows. Once Apollo 8 was in orbit, however, they could leave their couches if they wished. Astronaut Lovell, in charge of navigation, was the first to unbuckle. He left his couch, which was the middle

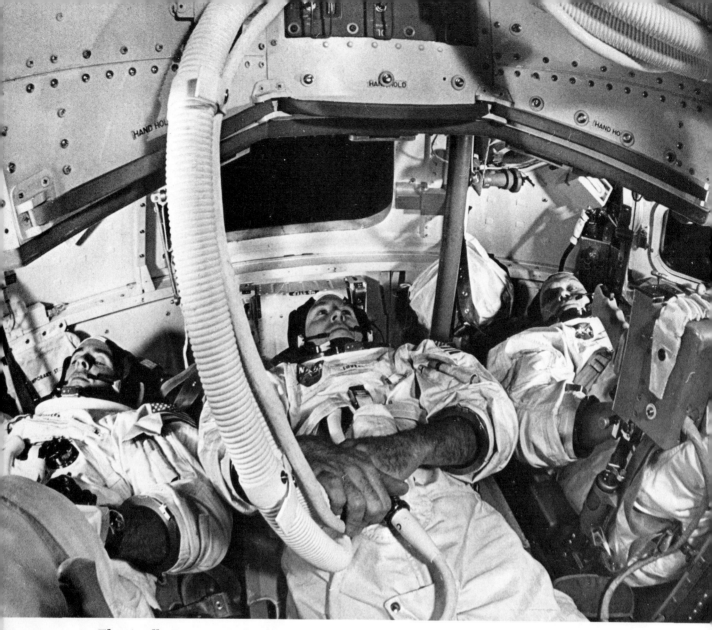

The Apollo 8 crew, Anders, Lovell, and Borman (left to right), train for their flight in the Apollo mission simulator.

one, and moved to a scanning telescope and a sextant fitted into the side of the cabin. During his previous trip into space as a Project Gemini astronaut, Lovell had remained strapped to his couch. Now he found himself floating "all over the place" in the weightless environment of the small Apollo cabin.

While Astronaut Lovell worked with his telescope and sextant, Mission Control in Houston had an important decision to make. Apollo 8 had successfully achieved a "parking" orbit a little more

than a hundred miles above the earth, but the spacecraft was still a long way from the moon. Moreover, getting to the moon presented many problems.

To achieve the velocity required to lift the spacecraft out of its earth orbit, the Saturn third-stage engine would have to be restarted. In addition, the spacecraft would have to be precisely aimed at a spot in space ahead of the moon because the moon would be moving around the earth while the spacecraft was moving toward it.

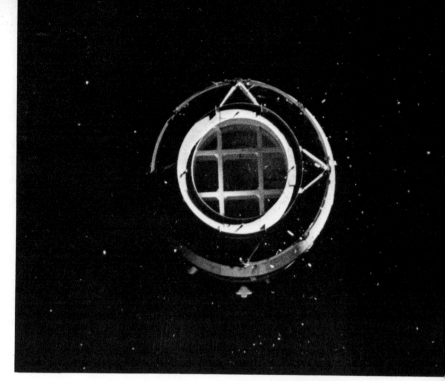

After separating from the Saturn third stage, the Apollo 8 astronauts photographed the orbiting rocket.

On its journey to the moon, Apollo 8 would be traveling through regions where radiation might be too high for safety. And if something should go wrong, it could take as long as three days for the Apollo astronauts to return to earth. Earlier astronauts had never been more than three hours away from an earth landing.

It is no wonder, then, that the Apollo 8 astronauts made a careful check of all the spacecraft's systems while they were still traveling safely around the earth. At the same time in Houston, NASA's Mission Director William C. Schneider, Director of Flight Operations Christopher C. Kraft, Jr., and Flight Director Clifford E. Charlesworth were analyzing data relayed to them from the spacecraft. The all-important decision came from Mission Control near the end of the second revolution: "Apollo 8, you are go for TLI [trans-lunar injection]."

At 10:41 A.M. high over Hawaii, the third-stage engine ignited with a burst of flame that was visible from the ground. The engine burned for five min-

utes and when it shut down, the Apollo 8 astronauts were heading for the moon at a speed of 24,226 miles an hour, faster than men had ever traveled before. From Christopher Kraft at the Manned Spacecraft Center came the message: "You're really on your way!"

Now that Apollo 8 had begun its long coast to the moon, the Saturn engine would not be needed again. Astronaut Borman turned a T-shaped handle that triggered explosive devices to separate the rocket from the spacecraft. "We have sep [separation] and looking good," the crew reported.

Instead of falling away, however, the spent rocket remained close to Apollo 8. Colonel Borman radioed to Houston: "It sure is staying close. It's spewing out from all sides like a huge water sprinkler. It's pretty spectacular." And Lovell added: "I am looking through the scanning telescope and I see millions of stars."

The rocket was venting unused fuel and sunlight-reflecting droplets of moisture surrounded it and Apollo 8. A

7

short firing of Apollo 8's control rockets, called thrusters, increased the distance between the spacecraft and the third stage to several thousand feet. The rocket remained visible, but it no longer endangered Apollo 8.

As they journeyed toward the moon, the astronauts turned their spacecraft to obtain a better view of the planet they were leaving behind. From Jim Lovell, 20,000 miles above the earth, came this enthusiastic description of a sight never before seen by human beings: "Boy, it's really hard to describe what this earth looks like. I'm looking out my center window, the round window, and the window is bigger than the earth is right now. I can clearly see the terminator [the line separating sunlight from darkness]. I can see most of South America all the way up to Central America, Yucatan, and the peninsula of Florida."

Astronaut Anders had some practical advice: "Tell the people in Tierra del Fuego [islands off the southern tip of South America] to put on their raincoats. Looks like a storm is out there."

A few minutes earlier, Anders, who was Apollo 8's systems engineer, had reported the readings on the personal

The Apollo 8 astronauts took this photograph of the earth after their spacecraft had begun its long coast toward the moon.

dosimeters worn by the three astronauts. These were small dialed instruments for measuring radiation that each man carried in a special pocket on the sleeve of his spacesuit. The dosimeters recorded less radiation than the astronauts would have received from a full dental x-ray, even though the spacecraft had passed through the thickest portion of the Van Allen radiation belts. The belts, roughly 2,300 and 11,000 miles from the earth, are regions of intense radiation.

Major Anders did have one complaint, however. "You might be interested to know the center window is pretty well fogged up," he radioed. Three of the spacecraft's five windows eventually became fogged. Later, technicians traced the trouble to sealing compound that leaked in the vacuum of space and formed a deposit between the three layers of glass in the windows.

Five and a half hours after lift-off Apollo 8 was almost 26,000 miles from the earth. The spacecraft still felt the pull of the earth's gravity, however. In fact, gravity had slowed the spacecraft's speed to 8,600 miles an hour. As it traveled toward the moon, Apollo 8 automatically made a slow, once-an-hour rotation. This prevented any one side of the craft from being exposed to the sun for too long at a time. The astronauts referred to the rotation as traveling in "barbecue mode."

After 11 hours and 60,000 miles of space flight, Apollo 8 began an important maneuver. It was a midcourse correction designed to put the spacecraft on an absolutely accurate flight path. But even more important, the midcourse correction was a test of Apollo's service propulsion system (SPS). The SPS en-

gine, located at the rear of the space capsule, was now the astronauts' only means of propulsion. It would be needed when they went into orbit around the moon and again when they headed back toward the earth. Their ability to start and shut down the engine was vital to the success of the Apollo 8 mission.

Because Apollo 8's flight path was such a good one, only a very slight midcourse correction was needed. Using data fed into their computer through a huge antenna at Goldstone, California, flight controllers at Houston decided that the SPS engine needed to burn for only 2.4 seconds, a "tweaking burn," as engineers call it. They radioed the information to the astronauts who started up the engine. The burn, short as it was, added 17 miles an hour to Apollo 8's speed. And equally important, it indicated that the engine was in perfect working order.

Shortly after the successful burn the capsule communicator at the Spacecraft Center sent a message to Apollo 8: "Okay, number one on the list of things is that the flight plan shows commander should hit the sack."

Because at least one of the astronauts had to be awake at all times to monitor the instrument panel and perform other necessary chores, the Apollo 8 crew was scheduled to sleep in shifts. After the message from Houston, Mission Commander Borman tried to go to sleep. He finally had to take a sleeping pill. Lovell and Anders had their sleep period when Borman awakened. They, too, had a restless "night."

In fact, more than sleeplessness bothered Colonel Borman during his first night in space. He was ill with nausea, vomiting, and diarrhea—symptoms of the highly contagious, 24-hour intestinal flu. To compound the problem, Lovell and Anders reported some nausea, especially when they left their couches to move around in the space capsule.

The report of a possible virus in space worried the men at the Mission Control Center. If the astronauts' health grew worse, they would have to return to earth following a single quick swing around the moon. After talking with Colonel Borman, Dr. Charles A. Berry, the astronauts' chief physician, prescribed some medication and recommended that the flight continue, at least for the time being. A close watch would be kept on medical data from the astronauts, however.

That afternoon Mission Control received incontestable evidence that the astronauts were feeling much better. From 139,000 miles in space the Apollo crew sent its first television presentation back to earth using a special 4½-pound camera.

"This program is coming to you from about halfway to the moon," announced Spacecraft Commander Borman. "We're about 31 hours, 21 minutes on the way and less than 40 hours from the moon."

Smiling and looking well, the astronauts showed their audience how they lived and worked in a space capsule. There was a shot of Frank Borman seated in his couch with his right hand on the control stick. Jim Lovell prepared dessert by injecting water into a bag of freeze-dried chocolate pudding and Bill Anders let go of a toothbrush to demonstrate how objects floated in the zero gravity of the spacecraft.

When the astronauts attempted to photograph the earth through a telescopic lens, their efforts were less successful. Mission Control received no picture and Capsule Communicator Michael Collins queried: "You don't have a lens cover on there, do you?"

Borman assured him that the cover had been removed.

As a last resort, the Apollo crew substituted a regular lens for the faulty telescopic one. It showed the earth as a blurred ball of bright light. This prompted Colonel Borman to tell the TV audience: "I certainly wish that we could show you the earth. It is a beautiful, beautiful view with predominantly blue background and just huge covers of white clouds." Before signing off he assured viewers: "We are all in very good shape."

Apollo 8's telecast was a remarkable engineering feat. In less than six-tenths of a second a TV signal flashed from a special antenna mounted on the rear of the spacecraft to NASA's receiving station at Goldstone, California. There technicians improved the picture and converted the signal to the frequencies used by commercial television before transmitting it to the Manned Spacecraft Center in Houston. From Houston the signal went to television networks in the United States and, by way of communications satellites, over the Atlantic and Pacific Oceans to TV stations in Europe, Hawaii, the Philippines and Japan.

Twenty-four hours later the astronauts sent a second telecast to the earth, now almost 200,000 miles away. This time, by using a filter with the telescopic lens, they were able to transmit a spectacular

For the TV audience, Astronaut Anders uses his toothbrush to demonstrate weightlessness in the gravity-free Apollo 8 capsule.

view of a bright, cloud-wrapped earth. "You're looking at yourselves as seen from 180,000 nautical miles out in space," announced Astronaut Borman.

Jim Lovell described the earth as it appeared from the spacecraft: "It's about as big as the end of my thumb. Waters are all sort of a royal blue; clouds, of course, are bright white. The reflection off the earth is much greater than the moon. The land areas are generally sort of dark brownish to light brown. What I keep imagining is, if I

were a traveler from another planet, what would I think about the earth at this altitude? Whether I think it would be inhabited?" He added: "I was just curious if I would land on the blue or the brown part."

"You better hope we land on the blue part," Borman told him. Apollo 8 was equipped for a water landing.

Only a few minutes after completing their second telecast, the astronauts passed into the moon's sphere of influence. They had traveled 200,000 miles into space and the moon was beginning to exert a stronger pull on Apollo 8 than the earth. It was the first time that men had come under the controlling influence of any celestial body other than the earth. Mission Control marked the occasion with a message: "Welcome to the moon's sphere!"

Apollo 8's speed had dropped to a low 2,223 miles an hour as it coasted

Apollo 8 within 70 miles of the lunar surface.

As Apollo 8 neared the end of its third day in space, Mission Control in Houston finished a check of all the equipment on the ground and in space that would be needed to put Apollo into orbit around the moon. "Everything looks go right now," the controllers told the astronauts.

The TV picture of the earth which the Apollo 8 crew transmitted from more than 120,-000 miles in space.

through space. Now the pull of the moon's gravity made the capsule move faster. As it sped toward the moon, Apollo 8's flight path needed only a very slight correction. This the astronauts accomplished by firing the spacecraft's maneuvering rockets for 11.8 seconds. The change in direction would bring

Later that evening Spacecraft Commander Borman had some surprising news for Mission Control. "We have yet to see the moon," he reported.

When asked what they could see, Astronaut Anders replied: "Nothing. It's like being on the inside of a submarine."

During most of the three-day journey

12

the spacecraft had been traveling with its windows turned away from the moon. Captain Lovell, the crew's navigator, had caught the only glimpse of the moon and that was through his telescope. The moon that he saw was approaching its first quarter. Most of the side facing the earth was dark. Because of its position between the earth and the sun, the moon was reflecting almost no light toward the earth. Earthshine, sunlight reflected from the earth, did light the moon's earth side slightly, however. Apollo 8's launch date had been selected to coincide with the best light for observation and photography on the moon, especially on the side away from the earth which would be in bright sunlight.

In one of his messages to flight controllers on the ground, Colonel Borman had cautioned: "The one thing we want is a perfect spacecraft before we consider this LOI [lunar orbit insertion] burn."

His concern was understandable. The single SPS engine had to function flawlessly to place Apollo 8 in the correct moon orbit. A similar flawless performance would be required from the engine when the space capsule left its moon orbit to return to earth. There was no way to rescue the astronauts if something went wrong. If the engine failed to burn for the proper length of time, Apollo 8 might go into an unstable orbit and crash on the moon. If the astronauts achieved a good orbit but were unable to leave it, their oxygen supply would be used up within a week. And if they missed their "re-entry corridor" on the way back, the results would be equally fatal.

The communication that the astro-

nauts were waiting for reached them at 3:54 A.M. on December 24. "Apollo 8, you are go for LOI," radioed the flight controllers. "You are riding the best bird we can find." The spacecraft was 2,939 miles from the moon and traveling at a speed of 3,759 miles an hour.

During the next 55 minutes the astronauts in Apollo 8 and the flight controllers on the ground made a last careful check of navigation data and spacecraft systems. Then it was time for final messages. Mission Control radioed: "One minute to LOS [loss of signal]. All systems go. Safe journey, guys!"

Astronaut Anders replied: "Thanks a lot, troops. We'll see you on the other side."

The last message that the astronauts received from Mission Control was a cheery: "You're go all the way!" Then Mission Control announced: "We've had a loss of signal with Apollo 8." The spacecraft had passed behind the moon and that body now blocked any radio signals coming from or to the capsule.

So far, the difficult and dangerous space flight had been amazingly successful. The three astronauts in Apollo 8 had traveled nearly a quarter of a million miles from the earth, much farther than the 850-mile record that Jim Lovell had set with Astronaut Edwin E. Aldrin, Jr. in Gemini 12. The Apollo 8 astronauts were the first to exchange the controlling influence of the earth for that of another celestial body. They were the first true space voyagers.

Behind the moon Apollo 8 was adding still another first to its list of accomplishments. After a successful 246.9-second firing of its SPS engine, the spacecraft went into an elliptical orbit around the moon. The orbit's pericynthion, or lowest point, was 70 miles above the lunar surface; its apocynthion, or highest point, was about 190 miles. (The terms pericynthion and apocynthion are derived from "Cynthia," one of the names of the Greek moon goddess, and they are used in connection with moon orbits. Perigee and apogee, which are derived from the Greek word meaning earth, are used when referring to the low and high points of earth orbits.) Apollo 8's pericynthion and apocynthion were exactly as planned. It was a momentous achievement.

One of the many photographs of the moon taken by Apollo 8 astronauts. The terrain at left is visible from the earth, but the terrain at right is hidden from direct view.

Christmas in Space

"Go ahead, Houston. Apollo 8."

Astronaut Lovell's matter-of-fact words, the first to be received from Apollo 8 since it had passed behind the moon and lost contact with the earth, assured Mission Control that the spacecraft was indeed in lunar orbit. It was 5:25 A.M. on the day before Christmas and the three astronauts had many things to tell the people on the ground. Jim Lovell did the describing: "The moon is essentially gray, no color. Looks like plaster of Paris. Sort of grayish beach sand. We can see quite a bit of detail."

While Apollo 8 was on the moon's sunlit far side and out of contact with Mission Control, the astronauts had viewed a moonscape that had never been seen before except in long-range photographs taken by unmanned Russian and American spacecraft. Now Apollo 8 was above the half of the moon facing the earth, an area illuminated partly by sunlight and partly by light reflected from the earth. The astronauts had spent many hours of their training studying the craters and "seas" on this side of the moon.

Jim Lovell continued his report: "The Sea of Fertility doesn't stand out as well here as it does back on earth. There's not much contrast between that and the surrounding craters." What he was describing was not a sea filled with water, but one of the moon's dusky regions to which seventeenth-century astronomers gave the Latin name *maria* because they looked like seas.

Lovell had no trouble locating a potential moon-landing site in a second dusky region, the Sea of Tranquillity. The sun was lower there and the resulting shadows helped the astronauts identify depths and heights on the lunar surface. "It's very easy to spot," Lovell said of the landing site. "I can see the rims of the crater including the white spot on the far side where the sun is shining into it.

"The craters are all rounded off," he continued. "There are quite a few of them. Some of them are newer. Looks like—especially the round ones—looks like they were hit by meteorites or projectiles of some sort.

"Langrenus is a huge crater. It's got a central core to it. The walls of the crater are terraced—about six or seven terraces on the way down. Coming up now in the Sea of Fertility are the old

friends Messier and Pickering [two craters] that I looked at so much on earth."

While Astronaut Lovell described the view to a fascinated audience at Mission Control and around the world, Apollo 8 was moving around the moon at 3,600 miles an hour. It was traveling nose-down; in that position the spacecraft's windows faced the lunar surface.

When Apollo 8 passed behind the moon, contact with the earth was lost for a second time. For the astronauts this was a busy period. As soon as they reached the earth side again, they were going to present their first telecast from the vicinity of the moon.

In millions of homes throughout the world, viewers gathered in front of TV sets to see the forbidding craters that pit the surface of the moon. As they pointed their camera at craters never before identified, the astronauts named them unofficially for friends and associates.

This photograph of the moon's far side, taken from Apollo 8, shows almost 100 miles of lunar horizon. The rugged terrain includes relatively new craters superimposed on older craters.

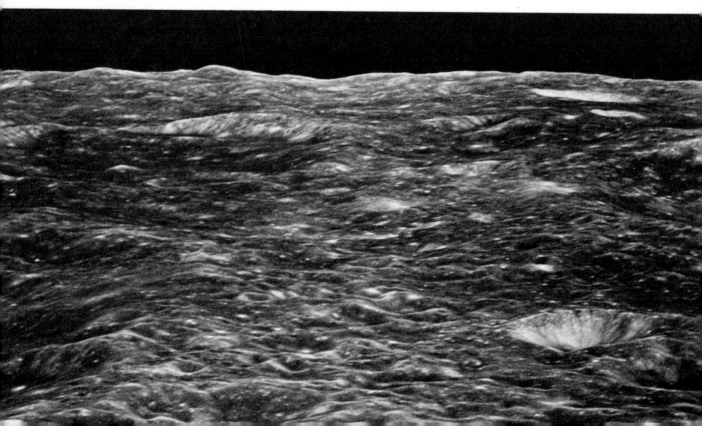

They also named three craters for themselves. "We are passing over the crater Borman," announced Bill Anders who was holding the TV camera. "And there's Anders over there and Lovell's right south of it."

During their third passage behind the moon, the astronauts fired Apollo 8's SPS engine for 9.6 seconds to place the spacecraft in a nearly circular orbit 70 miles above the lunar surface. Both the astronauts and the ground controllers were pleased with the flawless performance of the engine.

In addition to its television camera, Apollo 8 carried two Hasselblad still cameras and a 16-mm. movie camera along with an assortment of lenses. The astronauts had already taken still and motion pictures of the moon and from their new, lower orbit they took many more. Their color pictures were the first true color pictures of the lunar surface. From them scientists expected to learn more about the geography of the moon, especially of its far side. But after getting a close-up look at the moon's color, Astronaut Anders remarked: "All you really need is black and white film."

Shortly before 9:30 P.M. the astronauts put away the Hasselblads and the movie camera and took out their TV camera again. They were getting ready to transmit another TV program. On earth it was Christmas Eve and a bright quarter moon shone in the nighttime sky. "There's a beautiful moon out there," radioed Mission Control.

From Apollo 8 Frank Borman replied: "There's a beautiful earth out there."

"It depends on your point of view," agreed the ground controller.

While the TV audience viewed a

The terraced crater Langrenus photographed by Apollo 8 from about 150 miles above the lunar surface.

bright moon just 70 miles from the spacecraft, the three astronauts shared with them some of their own thoughts. "The moon is a different thing to each of us," Astronaut Borman remarked. "My own impression is that it is a vast, lonely forbidding type of existence, a great expanse of nothing, that looks rather like clouds and clouds of pumice stone. It certainly would not appear to be a very inviting place to live or work."

"My thoughts are very similar," said Jim Lovell. "The vast loneliness of the moon here is awe inspiring. . . . The earth from here is a grand oasis in the big vastness of space."

And Bill Anders told the TV audience: "I think the thing that has impressed me most is the lunar sunrises and sunsets that bring out the stark nature of the terrain."

During the telecast the Apollo crew identified the features of the lunar surface as they passed beneath the TV camera. Astronaut Borman provided

The Sea of Tranquillity as photographed by Apollo 8.

this description of an area in a sunlit portion of the moon: "What you see are the craters Casper and Gilbert. What you can't see are the small, bright impact craters that dominate the lunar surface. The horizon here is very, very stark. The sky is pitch black and the sun is white."

As the telecast from the moon drew to a close, Astronaut Anders said: "For all the people back on earth, the crew of Apollo 8 has a message we would like to send to you." He then began to read from the Bible's Book of Genesis: "In the beginning God created the heaven and the earth. And the earth was without form and void."

Taking turns, the astronauts read ten verses. Then Spacecraft Commander Borman said: "And from the crew of Apollo 8, we pause with good night, good luck, a merry Christmas, and God bless all of you—all of you on the good earth."

Early in the morning on Christmas Day, Apollo 8 prepared to head back toward the earth after orbiting the moon 10 times in 20 hours. The return journey began behind the moon where the spacecraft was once again out of radio contact with Mission Control. It was a tense time, both in the spacecraft and on the ground. If the SPS engine failed to start, the astronauts were doomed to remain in lunar orbit. But once again the engine fired perfectly to place the spacecraft on a trajectory that would bring it back to earth.

When radio contact was restored with Mission Control, a happy Astronaut Lovell announced the successful firing: "Please be informed, there is a Santa Claus."

From the capsule communicator at Mission Control came the cheery message: "I just would like to wish you all a very merry Christmas on behalf of everyone in the Control Center, and, I'm sure, everyone around the world. None of us ever expected a better Christmas than this one."

To that Astronaut Borman replied: "Thank everyone on the ground for us. It's pretty clear we wouldn't be anywhere if we didn't have them doing it or helping us out here."

As Apollo 8 sped toward the earth, its three-man crew settled down for a Christmas Day in space. They performed their assigned duties, exchanged long-range holiday greetings with their families and got some badly needed sleep.

About noon on Christmas Day Apollo 8, traveling at 3,000 miles an hour, moved through the equigravisphere— the region where the pull of the earth's gravity was equal to that of the moon. The moon was 39,000 miles away and the earth 202,000, when the spacecraft came under the controlling influence of the earth again. Because the earth is larger than the moon, the pull of the earth's gravity is stronger and extends farther into space.

During the afternoon the astronauts beamed their fifth telecast to the earth.

Spacecraft Commander Borman introduced the program by saying: "We've shown you scenes of the moon, scenes of the earth, and we thought we'd invite you into our home. It's been our home at least for four days."

Borman spoke from the commander's left-hand couch. Bill Anders, who was acting as cameraman, was on the right side of the spacecraft. In the middle, Jim Lovell's couch had been folded back and he was suspended in the gravity-free cabin with his head out of sight in the lower equipment bay. Instead of the bulky pressure suits they had worn when they left Cape Kennedy, the astronauts were wearing lightweight flight coveralls made of Beta cloth, a fire-resistant material. They had soft bootees on their feet. To keep the astronauts from floating around in the spacecraft, the bootees had soles made of Velcro which adhered to strips of the same material on the cabin floor. Their headgear consisted of soft strap-on hats equipped with microphones and earphones. The astronauts called them "Snoopy" hats because they resembled the headgear worn by the comic-strip beagle named Snoopy when he played the part of a World War I fighter pilot.

While Frank Borman supplied the commentary, Jim Lovell demonstrated how space travelers got their exercise. Lying on his back, he pulled on two stretchable cords attached to the wall near his feet. "He's working with an exercise devised and designed to keep the muscles in shape," explained Borman.

The camera moved to Apollo 8's computer, the device that stored navigation data and calculated signals for the space-

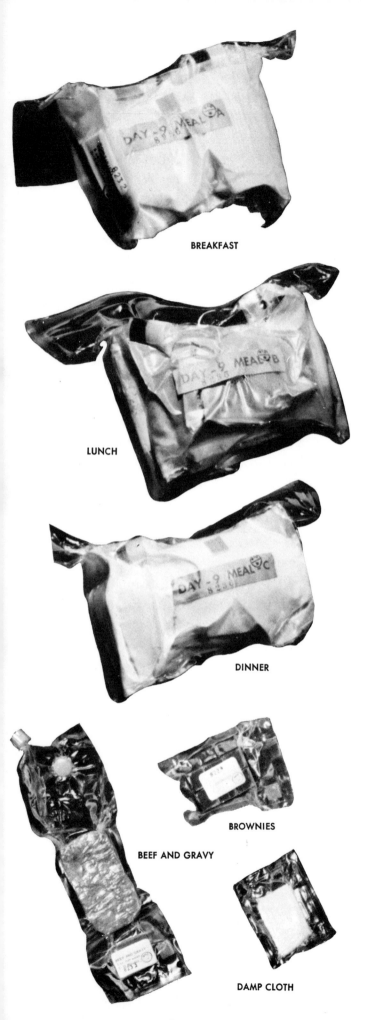

BREAKFAST

LUNCH

DINNER

BROWNIES

BEEF AND GRAVY

DAMP CLOTH

craft's SPS engine and thrusters. "You see, it is controlled by a DSKY [display and keyboard] or similar to a typewriter keyboard, and the things that come out of that are absolutely miraculous," Borman said.

Astronaut Lovell took over as cameraman while Bill Anders demonstrated how spacemen prepared their meals. "The food that we use is all dehydrated and comes prepackaged in vacuum-filled bags," remarked Borman. "The food is varied, generally pretty good," he added.

Astronaut Anders held several food packages. "Well, here we have some cocoa," he said. "It'll be good. I'll be adding about five ounces of hot water to that. These are little sugar cookies, some orange juice, corn chowder, chicken and gravy, and a little napkin to wipe your hands on when you're done."

Keeping the orange juice, Anders passed the other packages to Borman who began to describe the preparation of orange juice in space. "You can see that he is taking his scissors and cutting off the little nozzle that he is trying to insert the water gun into. The water gun dispenses a half-ounce of water per click." He continued: "Ordinarily, we let these drinks settle for 5 or 10 minutes, but Bill's going to eat one right— drink it right down. He's just opened another flap, and you'll see a little tube comes out. . . . And he drinks his delicious orange drink."

Freeze-dried foods such as those that the astronauts showed to their TV audience solve many of the problems of eating in space. They have little bulk, are easy to prepare and store, and last indefinitely without refrigeration. More-

Vacuum-packaged, freeze-dried food for the astronauts, with accessories.

over, when reconstituted with water, they have the same taste, texture, color, and nutritive value that they had before freeze-drying. Although they liked some of their prepacked meals better than others, the Apollo 8 crew found freeze-dried food quite palatable.

When food is freeze-dried, it is frozen and then exposed to a precise combination of vacuum and heat to draw off, as a vapor, any moisture in the food. This preserves the oils which give food its flavor.

In the Apollo spacecraft both hot and cold water were available for reconstituting the freeze-dried foods. Following instructions on the package, an astronaut added the proper amount of hot or cold water using the water gun demonstrated by Major Anders. He then kneaded the package to speed rehydration, opened one corner, and squeezed the contents into his mouth. When he finished eating, he broke an antimicrobial tablet into the package to prevent spoilage and placed the package in a waste storage bin.

Other food eaten by the astronauts was in the form of bite-sized pieces wrapped in plastic bags. Anything that would have a tendency to crumble was coated with a taste-free gelatin-like substance to hold it together. Crumbs floating around in a spacecraft could be a source of danger to the astronauts if they clogged vents, got into delicate instruments, or were inhaled.

After demonstrating how they prepared and ate food during a space journey, the astronauts showed the TV audience some of Apollo 8's navigation equipment in the lower equipment bay. "This is where we find out exactly where we are in space, what direction and how fast we're traveling," Jim Lovell, the spacecraft's navigator, explained. "And our computer takes the information and tells us how to maneuver to get home safely."

With a hearty "Merry Christmas" the astronauts brought their telecast to a close. Then they ate their Christmas dinner.

As a special treat, the Apollo crew's holiday meal was a real feast of turkey, cranberry sauce, and a grape drink. Unlike the food the astronauts had demonstrated on TV, the turkey was not dehydrated. Instead, it consisted of chunks of cooked turkey in gravy and the astronauts were able to eat it with a spoon. The gravy kept the turkey in the spoon until the astronauts could eat it. The meal came in foil-wrapped packages decorated with fireproof ribbon carrying the message "Merry Christmas." The astronauts reported that the turkey was delicious.

On Christmas night, Mission Control in Houston reported that Apollo 8 was right on course. However, the astronauts had two chances to adjust their flight path if that should prove necessary. "They'll be spending the next 37 hours looking very closely at that," said a NASA spokesman.

From thousands of miles above the earth the astronauts expressed their satisfaction with the spacecraft that had carried them around the moon. "If it keeps going this way for two more days, we have not only got the right spacecraft, we've got the best spacecraft," Colonel Borman radioed. About the condition of the astronauts he said: "We're all in good shape."

At 12:30 A.M. on December 26 Apollo 8 was 166,989 miles from the earth; its speed was close to 3,000 miles an hour. Ahead of the spacecraft lay the most severe test ever faced by a man-made vehicle because Apollo 8 was going to land without first orbiting the earth. As the spacecraft approached the earth and the pull of gravity became stronger, its speed would increase to 24,630 miles an hour, the fastest man had ever attempted to travel. Moreover, the capsule had to pass through a 30-mile-wide "re-entry corridor" at the outer edge of the atmosphere to enable gravity to pull it toward the earth at exactly the right angle. If it hit the earth's atmosphere at too steep an angle, heat from the resulting friction would burn up the spacecraft and its occupants. On the other hand, if the re-entry angle was too shallow, the resistance of the earth's atmosphere might bounce Apollo 8 back into space on an unplanned journey from which it would be unable to return.

However, re-entry was still many miles and more than a day away. In the meantime, the Apollo 8 crew carried out a schedule that included navigation exercises, sleep periods, meals, and conversations with controllers on the ground. When the spaceship reached the halfway point on its homeward journey, Astronaut Anders radioed: "Looking pretty good from here. How's it look down there?"

"Couldn't be better," was the reassuring answer.

In fact, Apollo 8's flight path was so accurate that a planned midcourse correction had been cancelled.

On the afternoon of December 26, the Apollo 8 astronauts presented a final TV program from space. This time they pointed their camera at the Western Hemisphere, wrapped in clouds in some areas, gleaming in sunlight in others.

"Looking down on the earth there from so far out in space, I think I must have the feeling that travelers on old sailing ships used to have," remarked Astronaut Anders. "We've gone on a very long voyage away from home and now we're headed back, and I have that feeling of being proud of the trip, but still happy to be going back to our home port."

"We'll see you back on that good earth very soon," Mission Commander Borman told the TV audience when Apollo 8 signed off for the last time.

Rest was now the most important activity on Apollo 8's flight plan. The astronauts wanted to be as alert as possible for the difficult re-entry and splashdown scheduled for early the next day. On the earth below the resting astronauts, a recovery force headed by the aircraft carrier *Yorktown* had assembled in the Pacific Ocean about one thousand miles southwest of Hawaii. That was where the spacecraft was scheduled to land in predawn darkness on Friday, December 27. In addition to the *Yorktown*, the U.S.S. *Cochrane* and the U.S.S. *Arlington* were on station in the landing area and three Air Force planes were standing by to drop pararescue teams if they were needed.

Weather in the landing area was reported to be good with scattered clouds at 2,000 feet and a broken layer of clouds at 6,000 feet. Seas were running four feet high and visibility was excellent.

Before splashdown, several busy,

tension-filled hours lay ahead for the Apollo crew. The astronauts began their landing preparations by stowing away all loose articles such as cameras and food bags that might fly around the capsule during re-entry. They also had to find a place for three bulky spacesuits and helmets because they were going to make a "shirt sleeve" re-entry in their flight coveralls. After looking around the small cabin, Frank Borman told Mission Control that they would put the suits under the couches and the helmets in food storage compartments. "Any stuff we have to take out of there we'll just stick in the suits," he explained.

Apollo 8, streaking toward the earth at more than 24,000 miles an hour, was over China when the astronauts fired small explosive charges to separate their space capsule from the service module behind it. The service module contained the SPS engine and the spacecraft's main oxygen supply. For the rest of their journey, the Apollo crew would be using oxygen from a reserve supply carried in the capsule itself. The spacecraft's systems would operate on power supplied by batteries.

Without the SPS engine the astronauts could no longer alter the spacecraft's course. However, they could use rockets built into the capsule to turn its blunt end down. They did this just before Apollo 8 entered the earth's atmosphere. The maneuver placed the thickest section of the capsule's heat shield where the resistance of the atmosphere was the greatest.

With its blunt end pointed toward the earth, Apollo 8 re-entered the earth's atmosphere after 6 days, 2 hours and 46 minutes of flight. Within seconds the spacecraft became red hot from the friction of the thickening air. The intense heat prevented all radio communication with the ground as the capsule plunged earthward.

Although Apollo 8 was cut off from radio contact, it was not out of sight. High over the Pacific an airline pilot enroute from Honolulu, Hawaii, to Sydney,

Apollo 8 re-entering the earth's atmosphere. A specially-equipped Air Force plane took the photograph.

Australia, saw the spacecraft's blazing re-entry. "We have Apollo 8 in sight," the pilot radioed. "He's making a red ball of fire followed by a long stream of white incandescent material."

How were the astronauts faring inside the "ball of fire" that was Apollo 8? Thanks to a protective coating of phenolic epoxy resin, a reinforced plastic, covering the space capsule, they hardly felt the heat. As the capsule's outer surface became hot, the phenolic epoxy resin charred and melted. This reaction dissipated the heat before it could penetrate to the astronauts. On the leading blunt end of the capsule where the temperature reached a blistering 5,000 degrees Fahrenheit, the resin was two inches thick.

Word that Apollo 8 had survived its fiery re-entry came from Astronaut Lovell. "We are in real good shape," he informed anxious ground controllers at the Houston Space Center when communications were restored.

Three minutes later Apollo 8's parachutes opened to steady the spacecraft and slow it down. The sky was still dark in the landing area, but the astronauts could see the parachutes in the flashing light of the spacecraft's stroboscopic beacon.

With its speed slowed to 20 miles an hour Apollo 8 splashed into the Pacific only three miles from the *Yorktown*. Almost at once the spacecraft turned upside down. Inside three uncomfortable astronauts dangled from the couches to which they were held by straps. Their discomfort was short-lived, however. As soon as large balloon-like bags carried in the capsule's tip had inflated, the craft righted itself.

After their successful journey to the moon, the Apollo 8 astronauts receive a congratulatory phone call from President Johnson.

Meanwhile, helicopters from the *York-town* had reached Apollo 8. While he circled overhead waiting for daylight, one of the pilots radioed the spacecraft to ask if the moon was really made of green cheese as the old saying describes it. "It's not made of green cheese at all," came the prompt answer from Apollo 8. "It's made of American cheese."

With the first light, frogmen jumped from the helicopters to attach a buoyant flotation collar around the spacecraft. They also helped the astronauts climb into the life rafts from which they were lifted into a helicopter for the short ride to the *Yorktown*. Later, a crane lifted the charred spacecraft onto the carrier's deck.

Doctors and technicians were waiting on the *Yorktown* to examine the astronauts and their craft. Both men and machine appeared to be in fine shape after the six-day, 590,000-mile Christmas journey to the moon.

Apollo 8's momentous achievement drew praise from many countries. Prime Minister Harold Wilson of Great Britain said: "This voyage is an important contribution to the expansion of mankind's knowledge of the universe." West Germany's Chancellor Kurt Kiesinger cabled: "I am glad this historic feat has come to a happy ending." The Soviet Union commended the "courage and skill of the astronauts."

Speaking for his countrymen, President Lyndon Johnson told the astronauts: "We all know that you men were supported by an elaborate technical apparatus, by many brilliant and devoted men and women here on the ground. We salute all of them as we salute you. . . . Well done!"

And indeed it was.

Seated beneath the plane flown by the Wright brothers and Lindbergh's Spirit of St. Louis, *members of Congress and their families listen as Astronauts Borman and Anders describe the Apollo 8 flight.*

Goal for Project Apollo

On May 25, 1961, when President John F. Kennedy delivered a special State of the Union message to Congress, he told the Senators and Representatives: "I believe that this nation should commit itself to achieving the goal, before this decade is out, of landing a man on the moon and returning him safely to earth. No single space project in this period will be more impressive to mankind, or more important for the long-range exploration of space, and none will be so difficult or expensive to accomplish."

The President's message marked the real beginning of the project that sent Apollo 8 to the moon. The Space Administration had already proposed sending astronauts on long flights in earth or lunar orbit, but NASA's Project Apollo was still in an early planning stage when the President made a manned landing on the moon a national goal. And the space age itself was not yet four years old.

It is generally agreed that the space age began on October 4, 1957, when the Soviet Union successfully launched its first Sputnik. That trail-blazing spacecraft carried 184 pounds of scientific instruments into orbit around the earth. And a month later Sputnik 2 went into orbit with a living passenger, a dog named "Laika."

Spurred by the achievements of the Soviet Union, the United States speeded

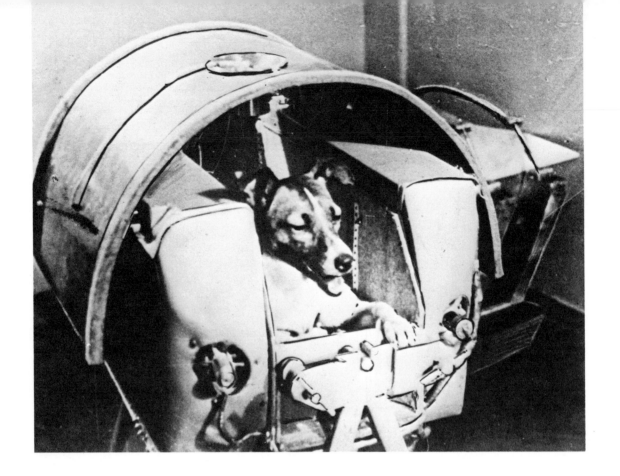

Above: *Laika just before her earth-orbital flight in Sputnik 2.*
Below: *One of the U.S.S.R.'s Vostok launch vehicles.*

up its own space program. The Army's Explorer 1, the first American earth satellite, went into orbit on January 31, 1958. Later that year, at President Dwight D. Eisenhower's request, Congress passed the National Aeronautics and Space Act. It outlined the space exploration objectives of the United States and created the National Aeronautics and Space Administration to carry them out.

The new Space Administration made plans for more unmanned space shots like Explorer 1 and for manned flights as well. The first United States manned space program was called Project Mercury. Its goals were to send an astronaut into orbit around the earth, to investigate man's ability to function in space, and to bring the astronaut and his spacecraft safely back again.

When President Kennedy issued his call for a manned landing on the moon before the end of the 1960s, Project Mercury had yet to send an astronaut into orbit. The Soviet Union had already accomplished this feat. On April 12, 1961, Cosmonaut Yuri Gagarin traveled around the earth in a Vostok spaceship. But Project Mercury had trained a group of seven astronauts and sent one of them on a successful suborbital flight up into space and back down again. And on February 20, 1962, Mercury Astronaut John Glenn made America's first manned orbital flight. He traveled around the earth three times. During the next fifteen months three other Mercury astronauts made successful orbital flights. On Mercury's final flight, Astronaut Gordon Cooper remained in space for 22 orbits.

Project Mercury was a very successful space program. It provided a good foundation for Project Apollo, but landing on the moon would be vastly more difficult than orbiting the earth. It would require more astronauts, a new spacecraft, a much more powerful booster rocket, and the development of new techniques for traveling and working in space.

To bridge the gap between the relatively simple Project Mercury and the extremely complicated Project Apollo, NASA inaugurated a new space program called Project Gemini. There were to be two astronauts on each Gemini mission. They would stay in space longer than the Mercury astronauts and would perform such difficult feats as docking, or linking, their spacecraft with other orbiting spacecraft.

While Project Mercury was still underway, NASA developed a larger version of the Mercury spacecraft for Project Gemini and began the training of additional astronauts. Even so, almost two years separated the last Mercury flight and Gemini 3, the first manned Gemini mission. Gemini 3 left Cape Kennedy's Pad 19 on March 23, 1965, and orbited the earth three times in a successful test of the new spacecraft and its systems.

There were four more Gemini flights during the remainder of 1965, each one designed to develop some system or activity that would be needed for Project Apollo. Gemini 4 remained in space for almost 98 hours. And during 23 minutes of that time, Astronaut Edward H. White II was outside the spacecraft. Extravehicular activity (EVA) would be necessary when Apollo astronauts explored the moon. Gemini 4 proved that it would be possible for them to leave their spacecraft and return to it later.

Gemini 5's flight lasted eight days. During that time the two-man crew performed a number of experiments including a simulated rendezvous, or meeting, with a second vehicle in space. Like EVA, the ability to rendezvous was essential to the success of Project Apollo. Gemini 6 provided further proof that a rendezvous in space was possible when Astronaut Walter M. Schirra guided his newly launched spacecraft to within a foot of the already orbiting Gemini 7.

The latter added to the accomplishments of the Gemini program by remaining in orbit for two full weeks.

Although its flight was cut short by a malfunctioning control system, Gemini 8 performed the first docking with another vehicle in space. Like EVA and rendezvous, docking was a maneuver vital to the success of Project Apollo.

Gemini's last four flights concentrated on perfecting EVA, rendezvous, and docking techniques. Gemini 12 brought the program to an end on November 15, 1966.

Astronaut White floats in space, secured to the Gemini 4 spacecraft by a 25-foot umbilical line and a 23-foot tether line wrapped together to form one cord. He holds a maneuvering gun.

During less than two years of manned space flight, Project Gemini's astronauts spent 970 hours in space. While orbiting the earth, they rendezvoused with other orbiting vehicles 10 times, completed 9 difficult docking maneuvers, and spent more than 12 hours outside their spacecraft. With three years remaining before the end of the 1960s, NASA was ready to move from the highly successful Gemini program to the vastly more complicated Apollo flights. It would mean more rendezvousing and docking, performed in lunar, rather than earth, orbit and extravehicular activity on the moon itself.

Before attempting to land men on the moon, NASA needed to know more about what they might find when they got there. In spite of its relative closeness to the earth, the moon has always been something of a mystery. For centuries men have speculated about what it is made of and where it came from.

Many ancient peoples believed in moon deities. The names they gave to their moon gods and goddesses have come down to us and we still use some of them when referring to the moon—for example, pericynthion and apocynthion. Another of the Greek names for the moon goddess was Selene and from this we get our word selenologist, a scientist who studies the physical features of the moon. The Latin word for moon is *luna.* It was one of the names the Romans gave to their moon goddess. Today, our word lunar means of, or pertaining to, the moon.

There have been many superstitions connected with the moon, and man has always held it in awe and sometimes

Gemini 7 photographed through the hatch window of Gemini 6 during rendezvous and station-keeping maneuvers.

This sixteenth-century woodcut shows astronomers searching the skies for clues to the movements of celestial bodies.

Using this telescope, Galileo discovered that the moon's surface was not smooth as earlier astronomers had thought.

fear. But man soon discovered it provided a reliable method of keeping time. As it travels around the earth, the moon's position in relation to the stars moves through a regular cycle every 29½ days. First there is the new moon which occurs when the moon is directly between the earth and the sun. The side of the moon facing the earth reflects no sunlight then and we cannot see it. Approximately a week later the moon has moved to a position that allows half of the side facing the earth to reflect sunlight. We call this "first quarter." After another week, we see a big, round full moon. In this phase almost all of the moon's bright side is facing the earth. From full the moon moves to its last quarter when we again see only half of the side facing the earth. Another new moon follows the last quarter and the cycle begins again.

A system of keeping time based on the phases of the moon is called a lunar calendar. Unfortunately, 12 lunar months add up to 354.4 days, or almost 11 days less than the 365 days that it takes the earth to make one revolution around the sun. For this reason a system of reckoning time based on the solar year gradually replaced the lunar calendar in most parts of the world.

Galileo Galilei, the Italian astronomer and physicist, was the first man to look

at the moon through a telescope. He did this in 1609 using a telescope that he had made himself. Galileo's telescope was not very powerful by modern standards, but it enabled him to see that the surface of the moon was not smooth as astronomers had thought. Instead, the moon was pitted with craters and dotted with highlands and mountains. Galileo reported his observations and soon other astronomers were studying the moon through telescopes. They were the first selenologists.

One of the early selenologists, German astronomer Johannes Hevelius, named the mountains that he saw on the moon for mountains on earth. Giovanni Ric-

cioli, an Italian selenologist, named several of the moon's craters after famous philosophers and scientists. The craters Copernicus and Tycho were named by Riccioli in honor of famous astronomers of the sixteenth century.

Because he thought that the dark areas he observed on the moon were seas, Riccioli gave them Latin names like Mare Imbrium (Sea of Showers) and Oceanus Procellarum (Ocean of Storms). Both Hevelius and Riccioli used Latin because it was the language of scholars and scientists in the seventeenth century when they lived. The custom of giving Latin names has persisted and lunar names are still officially given in Latin.

Today all names for newly discovered lunar features must be approved by the International Astronomical Union. In general, big features, such as the maria, are named for places and people, with only the names of dead people being used. The names that the Apollo 8 astronauts gave to several craters were unofficial.

In the years since Galileo and the other early selenologists first trained their primitive telescopes on the moon, we have learned that the moon has a diameter of 2,160 miles. This means that the moon's volume is $\frac{1}{50}$ that of the earth. In terms of area the surface of the moon covers nearly fifteen million square miles and all of it is dry land. The moon's gravity is only $\frac{1}{6}$ of the earth's, not enough to retain an atmosphere. As a result, the moon has no air, no clouds, and no moisture.

As mentioned before, the moon takes about 29½ days to go once around its orbit when measured against the stars.

However, because the earth and moon are moving together around the earth's orbit, it takes only a little over 27 days for the moon to make a complete orbit with respect to the sun. During this time its distance from the earth varies from 221,463 miles to 252,710 miles.

While the moon is traveling around the earth once, it is also rotating on its axis once. In a lunar day there are about 14 days of sunshine and about 14 days of darkness. During the hours of sunlight, temperatures on the moon may climb as high as 250 degrees Fah-

grams, called Ranger, spacecraft carrying six television cameras each returned pictures of the lunar surface before making a hard, or crash, landing.

Ranger was a complicated space program that experienced several failures before accomplishing its objective. Ranger 6, launched on January 30, 1964, was the first to reach the moon, but it failed to send back any pictures. The next three Rangers more than made up for the early failures, however. Ranger 7 returned 4,316 excellent photographs of a possible Apollo landing site near

When Surveyor 3 landed it bounced. Over two years later, the Apollo 12 astronauts took this close-up of one of the craft's footpads and the imprint it left in the lunar soil.

renheit near the lunar equator. During darkness, on the other hand, temperatures drop to a freezing 280 degrees below zero.

To add to these and other facts already known about the moon, NASA developed a series of unmanned spacecraft to precede the astronauts to that body. The spacecraft were designed to send photographs and other information back to earth. In the first of these pro-

the lunar equator. NASA shared the photos with the world's astronomers and geologists. Ranger 8 sent back 7,162 photographs of a second potential landing area. Ranger 9, launched on March 21, 1965, and the last of the series, returned another 5,814 photos.

From Ranger, NASA learned that the photographed areas, all of them near the lunar equator, were smoother than expected, and therefore, less hazardous for a manned landing. Questions about the hardness of the lunar surface remained, however, and another program, called Surveyor, was developed to provide some answers.

Unlike Ranger spacecraft which crashed on the moon, Surveyors were designed to make a controlled, or soft, landing in an area under consideration as an Apollo landing site. The soft landing was made possible by a rocket engine which slowed the Surveyor's speed as it approached the moon. Then smaller engines lowered the craft gently until its three footpads rested on the lunar surface.

Surveyor 1, launched in June, 1966, made the first controlled landing on the moon. It sent back the first pictures in color taken on the moon itself. By examining photos that showed one of the Surveyor's footpads, scientists were able to determine that the pad had sunk no more than one or two inches below the surface. This meant that if the Apollo spacecraft had landed there, the astronauts would not have been in danger of sinking in deep dust.

In addition to sending back pictures, another Surveyor actually tested the moon's soil using a small motor-driven scoop called a surface sampler. On command from the earth, the surface sampler pounded the lunar surface, dug into it, and moved small amounts of lunar soil from one place to another while measuring devices recorded the results which were transmitted back to earth.

The first chemical analysis of lunar soil was performed by Surveyor 5. With a tool called an alpha back-scatterer, it discovered that the moon's soil resembled the earth's basaltic rock. Surveyor 5 also detected magnetic particles on the moon and its television camera sent back many excellent photos.

Surveyor 6 repeated Surveyor 5's mission, but in another possible Apollo landing area. When its work was finished, NASA technicians re-ignited its engine by remote control and the craft rose 10 feet from the lunar surface. That was high enough to prove that a takeoff from the moon was possible. Surveyor 6 was the first United States spacecraft to

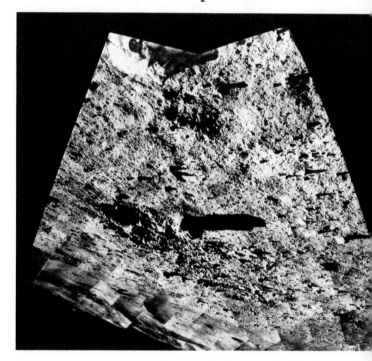

This panoramic view of one of the moon's highland regions is a mosaic of 212 pictures of the moon taken by Surveyor 7's television camera.

attempt a takeoff from another celestial body.

Because several Apollo landing sites had already been investigated, NASA sent Surveyor 7 to a rugged region near the crater Tycho. It sent back information on one of the moon's highlands. The Surveyor 7 launch on January 7, 1968, was the last in the Surveyor series.

While Surveyors were landing on the moon's surface, other spacecraft, called Lunar Orbiters, were traveling in a low orbit around the moon to gather information on favorable landing sites for later Surveyors and for the Apollo astronauts. The five Lunar Orbiters launched between August, 1966, and August, 1967, were flying photographic laboratories. They carried two cameras, one for wide-angle and another for telephoto coverage, a film processor, and a device for electronically transmitting the photos back to earth. All of the photographic equipment carried by an Orbiter weighed less than 150 pounds.

Lunar Orbiters concentrated on the moon's equatorial region because that area seemed most suitable for an Apollo landing, but they covered other sections as well. When the project ended, 99 per cent of the moon had been photographed. Moreover, the photographs showed much more detail than could be seen with the very best of earthbound telescopes. In addition to transmitting a great many excellent pictures of the moon's surface, Lunar Orbiters gathered data on the moon's environment and its gravitational field.

Like Ranger and Surveyor, Lunar Orbiter provided much useful information for the Apollo astronauts and for the world's selenologists. Some big questions about the moon remained, however. One of the questions that still puzzled scientists had to do with the origin of the moon. Where did the moon come from? Was it a former planet that billions of years ago wandered too close to the earth and got caught in the earth's gravitational field? Or was the moon created at the same time as the earth? Or could the moon be a former part of the earth that broke away long ago?

If the moon was once a planet, it may have had an atmosphere with rainfall and rivers, lakes and oceans. Or it may have caught a huge splash of water from the earth's oceans when it passed close to the earth. The presence of water at some time in the past would account for some of the features on the moon, especially the lunar rills—wandering trenches which resemble dried up stream bottoms.

Some scientists believe that both the earth and the moon may have been formed by the condensation of cosmic matter, a process that may also have created the rest of our solar system. Another theory, now questioned, is that at some time in the past a large chunk of earth broke away and formed the moon. It has been suggested that the breakaway material came from the area of the Pacific Ocean, leaving behind a huge hole that became the Pacific basin.

Another unanswered question about the moon concerns its internal temperature. Is it a cold, dead mass, or does it have a molten interior which produces volcanic activity similar to that on earth? In general scientists who believe that the moon is an old planet caught in the earth's gravitation field also believe that it is a cold body. Those who think the moon was formed at the same time as the earth, or was once a part of the earth, also think that it is, or was, hot. They point to the basalt-like surface material identified by Surveyor 5 as proof of volcanic activity on the moon. On the earth basalt is of volcanic origin. Moreover, many of the moon's craters resemble volcanic craters on earth.

Lunar craters are shallow depressions whose rocky rims are higher than the surrounding surface. They measure anywhere from a few inches to more than a hundred miles in diameter and there are a great many of them. While some of the moon's craters appear to be of volcanic origin, others resemble the huge Meteor Crater in Arizona. It was created when a big meteor crashed into the earth in the distant past. A number of selenologists think that meteors are responsible for the moon's craters and perhaps for the lunar seas as well. In the latter case, the meteors would have to be very large.

Selenologists have been arguing about the moon's craters for years. Many of them are inclined to accept the theory that both volcanism and the impact of meteors may be responsible for the craters of the moon.

When President Kennedy selected the moon as the target for the nation's first extraterrestrial exploration, he was aware of the fact that the moon was closer than the planets and easier to reach. But he also knew that exploring the moon would provide answers to many important questions about that body. Moreover, it was likely that exploring the moon and examining its surface materials would provide information about the origin of the earth and the rest of the solar system. If Project Apollo attained its goal, the world's scientists would acquire a greater understanding of the universe we live in.

Part of the crater Copernicus photographed by Lunar Orbiter 5.

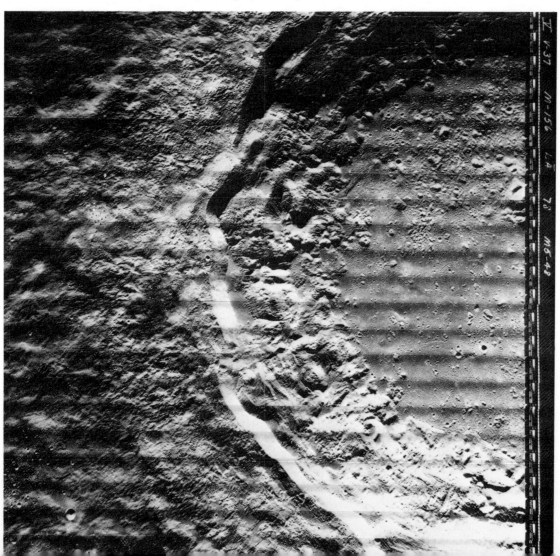

Preparing for the Big Adventure

In 1865 a popular French author named Jules Verne wrote a story about a fictitious journey to the moon. In the story, which he called *From the Earth to the Moon,* Verne described how a spaceship traveled to the moon from a launching pad in southern Florida not far from the present John F. Kennedy Space Center.

Although Verne had no scientific training he correctly described how weightlessness affected the spacecraft's three passengers, and he devised an ingenious system of rockets to steer the craft during its journey. Not all of Verne's inventions were scientifically feasible, however. He launched his bullet-shaped spacecraft from a huge, 900-foot-long cannon, a blast-off that would surely have killed the prospective

space travelers before they ever left Florida.

A hundred years later, when Project Apollo began to make plans for landing astronauts on the moon, one of the first problems that had to be solved was how to get them there. Like the travelers in Jules Verne's story, the astronauts had somehow to be lifted into space.

If NASA were to build an enormously powerful rocket, the Apollo spaceship could be sent directly to the moon. But such a rocket would have to have a thrust, or pushing power, of at least 12 million pounds, and it was doubtful if one could be developed before 1970.

Smaller rockets would be easier to produce, but they couldn't carry a spacecraft all the way to the moon. Instead,

In his book From the Earth to the Moon, *Jules Verne devised an ingenious system of rockets to power a mooncraft.*

they would have to boost a capsule and two or more fuel-carrying sections into an earth orbit where they would be assembled and launched on the long journey to the lunar surface.

Another possible method of getting to the moon was to use a fairly large rocket to send a spaceship carrying a landing craft into lunar orbit. From there the landing craft would carry astronauts to the moon's surface. Later it would bring them back to the orbiting mother ship which would then return to earth.

For a time it appeared that NASA would choose to assemble its moonship in earth orbit. This meant that the en-

tire spacecraft would have to land on the moon and take off again when the astronauts had finished exploring. To Dr. John C. Houbolt, one of NASA's aeronautical engineers, landing a heavy spacecraft on the moon was not the best method of getting there. Instead, he favored the lunar-orbit rendezvous method. Dr. Houbolt pointed out that a small landing craft would be much easier to guide to the lunar surface. And it would require less rocket power for its takeoff from the moon. Moreover, the lunar-orbit rendezvous method would eliminate the difficult step of assembling spacecraft sections in earth orbit.

A less practical way of getting to the moon described by a writer in the seventeenth century.

During the summer of 1962, NASA made an important decision. Project Apollo would use the lunar-orbit rendezvous method to reach the moon. The Space Administration was already at work on a powerful new family of boosters called Saturn. The three stages of the largest version of the Saturn would be able to produce 8,700,000 pounds of thrust. That was enough to launch a spacecraft into lunar orbit.

NASA's Saturn rockets were under development in its George C. Marshall Space Flight Center at Huntsville, Alabama. The director of the Center, Dr. Wernher von Braun, was a former German rocket scientist who came to the United States after World War II. During the war he had worked on the V-2 rockets that the German army launched against Great Britain. In the United States von Braun and some of his former colleagues in the V-2 project launched captured V-2s for the United States Army. In America, however, instead of the explosives that they had delivered during the war, the V-2s carried scientific instruments.

From the V-2 project von Braun and his team of specialists moved on to the development of new rockets. One of their rockets, the Redstone, was used in the suborbital Mercury flights, and others successfully boosted some of NASA's unmanned capsules into space.

America's early rockets were comparatively small ones. The Soviet Union, on the other hand, had concentrated on building large rockets capable of carrying heavy loads into space. Dr. von Braun thought that the United States should build large rockets too, and in 1958 he received permission to begin work on the Saturns that were to play such an important part in Project Apollo.

There have been three boosters in the Saturn family. Saturn 1, the first to be developed, was considerably more powerful than any previous American booster. Its two stages, or sections, could lift 22,000 pounds into a low earth orbit.

Saturn 1B was even more powerful than the earlier Saturn 1. It could lift

At Nasa's Marshall Space Flight Center, the first stage of a Saturn 5 launch vehicle is lifted into position for test firings.

40,000 pounds into a low earth orbit. The 1B used an improved version of the Saturn 1 first stage and an entirely new second stage. Each of the stages had its own rocket engines and fuel supply. The powerful single engine of the Saturn 1B's second stage burned a cryogenic, or ultra-low-temperature, fuel. This was composed of liquid hydrogen at 423 degrees Fahrenheit below zero and liquid oxygen at 297 degrees below zero. In order to maintain such low temperatures, fuel tanks had to be insulated and all pipes, valves, and other components of the fuel system had to be insulated as well. What made the extra engineering worthwhile was the fact that liquid hydrogen in combination with liquid oxygen is a light fuel that produces a great deal of energy for every pound of its weight.

Saturn 5 towers to a height of 282

Three Apollo astronauts enter the Apollo mission simulator. The double exposure also shows them manning their stations inside the simulator.

feet, as high as a 28-story building. The five engines of its 138-foot-long first stage generate a total thrust of 7.5 million pounds. They burn a combination of refined kerosene and liquid hydrogen which are carried in two separate tanks. Together the tanks hold 534,000 gallons, but the first-stage engines burn fuel at the rate of 3,500 gallons a second. Two and a half minutes after blast-off the vast tanks are almost empty and the five engines shut down.

Five second-stage engines take over from the first stage. They are smaller than the first-stage engines, burn super-cold liquid hydrogen and liquid oxygen, and produce 1,125,000 pounds of thrust.

The Saturn 5 second stage is designed to reach a distance of about one hundred miles above the surface of the earth.

Saturn 5's third stage is the same as the Saturn 1B second stage. Its versatile engine, which can produce up to 225,000 pounds of thrust, has two important assignments during a moon flight. After the second-stage engines exhaust their fuel supply and shut down, the third-stage engine puts the spacecraft into earth orbit. Later it is re-ignited to start the spacecraft on the long journey to the moon.

While Wernher von Braun and his colleagues were developing the big Sat-

Astronaut Michael Collins practices a rendezvous and docking maneuver in the Apollo mission simulator.

urn rockets, work was under way on the capsule that the Saturn would boost into space. Unlike the Gemini capsule, which was an enlarged version of the older Mercury capsule, the Apollo capsule incorporated a great many new features in its three modules, or sections.

Working closely with NASA, the Space Division of the North American Rockwell Corporation developed the Apollo spacecraft's command and service modules. The corporation's designers and technicians produced a command module to serve as both living and working quarters for a three-man Apollo crew. During a moon mission it would be their bedroom, kitchen, dining room, cockpit, office, laboratory, and radio station.

Although it was designed to hold three astronauts, the cone-shaped command module's diameter was only 12 feet, 10 inches. It was 10 feet, 7 inches tall. Most of the module's area was taken up by the three reclining couches in which the astronauts would spend a great deal of time, but, unlike the Mercury and Gemini capsules, there was also room for them to stand and move around. The couches rested on shock-absorbing struts. Instrument panels and consoles lined the walls. Additional equipment was stored in bays, or cupboards. The module had two side windows, a hatch window, and two rendezvous windows which faced its nose.

Double walls protected the astronauts from the hostile environment of space. The outer wall was of steel and it was covered by the spacecraft's heat shield. An inner aluminum wall surrounded the pressurized work and living area. During flight the temperature inside the module would remain a comfortable 70 to 75 degrees Fahrenheit.

Apollo's cylindrical service module, located directly behind the command module, was designed to house the spacecraft's support systems. These included its electrical power and oxygen supplies, as well as its service propulsion system (SPS). Controlled by a computer, the SPS engine was the one that would put the Apollo spacecraft into orbit around the moon and bring it back to earth again. If the spacecraft should wander off course, it would provide the power for a change of direction. The engine, which delivered 20,500 pounds

of thrust, burned a blended hydrazine fuel. The engine started when nitrogen tetroxide oxidizer was added to the hydrazine and no sparkplug was needed. In tests the SPS engine had been restarted as many as 50 times and it had burned for a total of 12½ minutes, more starts and more burning than would be needed for its important Apollo assignments.

Although the SPS engine was normally controlled by a computer, the astronauts themselves could take over if the computer failed. On the journey back from the moon, they would separate the service module with its SPS engine from the command module and jettison it before re-entering the earth's atmosphere.

At blast-off the service module would be sitting atop the Saturn 5 booster with a 28-foot-tall adaptor section connecting the two. In addition to serving as a connection, the adaptor had another important function. During the first part of the mission it would house Apollo's remarkable lunar module, or LM, the craft that would actually touch down on the moon's surface.

The LM was designed to fly only in space. It would travel into space in the adaptor and remain there until the spacecraft left its earth orbit and headed for the moon. Then the astronauts were scheduled to separate the command and service modules from the adaptor and the Saturn's third stage. They were to turn the spacecraft around and dock with the LM, separate it from the adaptor and, still docked with the LM, resume their journey to the moon.

Because the LM would fly only in space, it did not have to be streamlined.

Apollo astronauts use the lunar module trainer to practice moon landings and takeoffs.

The inverted ascent stage of a lunar module is lowered onto a command module during a docking test.

Instead, a welter of antennas protruded from its bug-like body. Four spindly legs and the location of its windows and hatch added to the craft's bug-like appearance. Anyone seeing the LM understood at once why it was called "the bug."

The LM might look less sophisticated than other spacecraft, but in fact it was the most complex vehicle ever made. Built by Grumman Aircraft Engineering Corporation, it was designed to carry two astronauts from an Apollo spacecraft in lunar orbit to the surface of the moon, serve as their living quarters and base of operations while they were on the moon, and then return them to the orbiting spacecraft.

The LM's lower portion contained the engine that lowered the landing craft to the surface of the moon, a descent that could be slowed to three miles an hour. In the upper stage were a cabin for the two astronauts and an ascent engine to lift it back to the orbiting mother ship. The lower stage was to serve as a launch platform for the upper stage and remain behind on the moon.

Who was going to use the LM and the other complex equipment designed for Project Apollo? NASA had a large group of astronauts from which to choose. A few of the original seven Mercury astronauts were still available for space flights and most of the Gemini astronauts had also transferred to Project Apollo. In addition, NASA had added several new groups of astronauts especially for the moon landing program.

With Project Apollo, scientists joined the ranks of the astronauts for the first time. Until 1965, NASA had selected its astronauts exclusively from the nation's best-qualified military and civilian test pilots. These pioneer astronauts tested Mercury and Gemini spacecraft and equipment much as they would have tested a complex new airplane. Project Apollo, however, added a new dimension to the astronauts' tasks. In addition to flying spacecraft, Apollo astronauts were going to explore the moon. This was a job for scientists, and NASA recruited physicists, geologists, astronomers, and physicians, as well as test pilots for Project Apollo. However, as part of their training, the new scientist-astronauts were expected to become fully qualified pilots.

Standards for scientist-astronauts were as high as those for pilot-astronauts. The scientists had to be United States citizens, under 35 years of age, no taller than six feet, in excellent physical and mental condition, and holders of an advanced degree in science or medicine. Of the 1,492 scientists who answered NASA's first call for applicants in 1965, all but 16 were eliminated before the last series of tests and only six finally qualified for the Apollo program. Eleven more scientist-astronauts were selected in 1967. The scientist-astronauts joined the veteran astronauts of Projects Mercury and Gemini and newly selected pilot-astronauts in an intensive training program for Project Apollo.

Under the direction of Donald K. Slayton, a former Project Mercury astronaut who became the Manned Spacecraft Center's director of flight-crew operations, the astronauts studied every detail of the Apollo spacecraft. They traveled to North American Rockwell's

At the manufacturer's plant, astronauts contribute to critical reviews of the design of the Apollo spacecraft.

plant in California where the command and service modules were being assembled and to the Grumman Engineering Corporation's plant in New York where work was underway on the lunar module. They also watched numerous tests of spacecraft parts. In classrooms they studied flight mechanics, navigation, and computer science. Their goal was to learn to operate the Apollo spacecraft as proficiently as possible.

To prepare for the experiments that they would conduct during the journey to the moon and on the moon itself, the astronauts studied geology, astronomy, meteorology, and physics of the upper atmosphere. The information that they acquired would also help them to report

NASA scientists assemble photographs of the moon's surface taken by a Lunar Orbiter to form a mosaic, which the astronauts can study in their training for Apollo missions.

accurately on their observations during a lunar mission.

The astronauts would be exposed to unusual stresses during the rapid acceleration of blast-off and the equally rapid deceleration that occurs when a spacecraft re-enters the earth's atmosphere and they trained for that, too. They used a centrifuge, a machine that rotates at a high speed. By riding in the whirling centrifuge at the Manned Spacecraft Center, the astronauts could prepare for the stresses of launch and re-entry. They also learned how much work they would be able to do under similar conditions during a space flight.

True weightlessness is hard to reproduce on earth, but the astronauts had to be prepared for the weightlessness that they would experience in space and, to a lesser extent, on the moon. If an airplane is flown along a path that resembles an inverted U, its passengers will be weightless for 30 seconds or more. The astronauts took advantage of this fact, using one of the Air Force's four-engine jet aircraft. They also worked underwater because the natural buoyancy of water partially reproduces the effects of weightlessness.

Although Apollo spacecraft were designed to land on water, an emergency

During training, Apollo astronauts experience weightlessness for a short period in a jet aircraft.

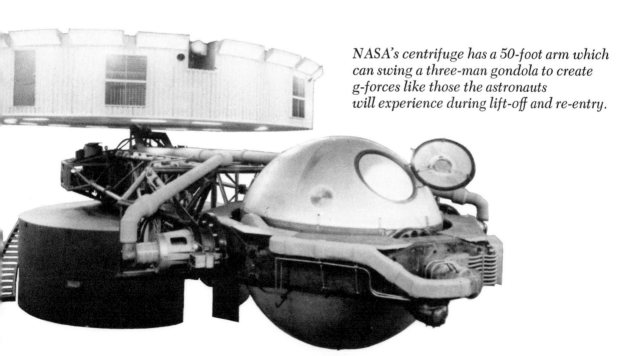

NASA's centrifuge has a 50-foot arm which can swing a three-man gondola to create g-forces like those the astronauts will experience during lift-off and re-entry.

could force one to land almost anywhere. In that case the astronauts might find themselves miles from help in a desert, a jungle, or a mountainous area. Survival training, in the form of lectures, demonstrations, and actual practice, taught the astronauts how to find food and shelter no matter where they landed. They were also prepared for an emergency landing at sea far from the nearest recovery ship.

When an astronaut received an assignment to a three-man Apollo crew, he began to prepare for a specific mission. Some of his special training took place in elaborate machines called simulators. One of NASA's simulators exactly duplicated the command module of the Apollo spacecraft. Another duplicated the lunar module. Neither simulator ever left the ground, but they contained all the instrument panels, controls, switches, and equipment of the original craft. An astronaut could "fly" an entire mission in these simulators, from 60 seconds before launch to re-entry. Moreover, almost anything he might hear or see on a real mission could be duplicated. The simulators were not able to reproduce the sensation of weightless-

An engineer checks the scale of craters on a lunar map which is part of the lunar-orbit and landing-approach simulator. The simulator presents the astronaut-pilot with the lunar features that he would see during an approach to a moon landing.

Astronaut Neil Armstrong pilots the lunar-landing training vehicle.

ness and the stresses of launch and re-entry. But they could present the astronaut with a variety of emergency situations to give him practice in handling in-flight problems.

In another of NASA's simulators the astronauts could practice docking and undocking with a second craft. And in a simulator called a lunar-landing training vehicle they could actually fly a little. It was designed to give them practice for the critical landing on the moon.

An astronaut's preparation included physical fitness as well as training in classrooms, laboratories, and flight sim-ulators because any astronaut who went to the moon would have to be in top condition. The physical-fitness program was an informal one. "We have not said you're going to run so many miles a day, you're going to do so many sit-ups a day," explained Dr. Berry, the astronauts' physican. "We have said only it's a responsibility of every astronaut to keep himself in good, sound physical fitness. Some like to swim, some like handball. They can have their pick."

If Project Apollo was to be successful, the astronauts, like the Saturn booster and the spacecraft, would have to be the very best that the country could produce.

"Fire in the Cockpit!"

The first flight of a new spacecraft or launch vehicle is always an exciting occasion. In February, 1966, excitement at Cape Kennedy was doubly high because both the Apollo spacecraft and the Saturn 1B booster were ready for testing. It was to be a joint test and a very important one. A successful flight would mean that NASA was well on the way to placing a man on the moon before 1970. On the other hand, if either the unmanned spacecraft or the Saturn developed serious problems, time-consuming redesigning might be necessary.

Anxious space officials had to wait through three days of heavy rain before the crucial test flight could be launched. On February 26 trouble in the Saturn's

pressure system almost caused another postponement. It was finally corrected, however, and the huge rocket roared off the launching pad, a bright orange flame shooting from its tail. The mooncraft that it carried weighed 37,400 pounds, the heaviest load yet lifted into space.

Two and a half minutes after launch, at an altitude of 33 miles, the Saturn's first stage shut down right on schedule and separated from the second stage. The second-stage engine burned for 7½ minutes before exhausting its fuel and shutting down. When that stage dropped off, the engine in the spacecraft's service module fired up to send the capsule hurtling back into the atmosphere at a speed that exceeded 18,000

Carrying an unmanned Apollo spacecraft, a Saturn 1B rocket thunders aloft on the first flight for the spacecraft and the rocket.

miles an hour. The heat-blackened craft landed in the Atlantic Ocean only 35 miles from where the carrier *Boxer* was waiting to pick it up.

During the 40-minute test the Saturn had functioned perfectly. The Apollo spacecraft's engine had started up in the vacuum of space and its heat shield successfully withstood a blistering 5,000-degree re-entry. "This was a test of great importance," Dr. George E. Mueller, the director of NASA's manned space program, announced happily. "It was the first step of the manned Apollo program to the moon."

On August 25, 1966, a Saturn 1B launched a second Apollo spacecraft on a suborbital test flight. This time the capsule traveled three quarters of the way around the earth to a landing in the Pacific Ocean southeast of Wake Island. During its 94-minute journey it reached an altitude of 706 miles.

When it pushed through the earth's thickening atmosphere during re-entry, the test craft had to endure searing temperatures. Its heat shield was equal to the test, however, and Dr. Mueller told a post-launch press conference: "The results of the flight were extremely gratifying. We did carry out all of the mission's objectives."

After being plucked from the Pacific by the carrier *Hornet,* the spacecraft was taken to California where it was examined with great care by engineers from NASA and North American Rockwell. Whether the next Apollo flight would be a manned one depended upon the results of that examination. The decision: The next Apollo flight would be manned. It was scheduled for November 15, 1966.

No one was more pleased with NASA's decision than Astronauts Virgil I. Grissom, Edward H. White II, and Roger B. Chaffee. They had been chosen as the first Apollo crew and were already in training for a flight which was to carry them into orbit around the earth.

Grissom, an Air Force lieutenant colonel, was a veteran astronaut. He had made a suborbital flight in a Mercury capsule in 1961 and commanded the first manned Gemini flight in 1965. Air Force Lieutenant Colonel Edward H. White II became the first astronaut to walk in space during the Gemini 4 flight. For Navy Lieutenant Commander Roger Chaffee, the pioneer manned Apollo mission would be a first trip into space.

The three astronauts trained in a simulator that duplicated the Apollo command module and practiced the many procedures they would use during their space journey. Meanwhile their capsule was undergoing many checks. It had already been tested by North American Rockwell, the company that manufactured it. Then, after being delivered to Cape Kennedy in a special cargo-carrying airplane called a Super Guppy, it underwent another series of tests. Some of the tests at the Cape took place in a chamber that reproduced the conditions found at altitudes more than 200,000 feet above the earth. This was done to make sure that the capsule's systems would operate under conditions approximating those to be found in space.

The astronauts who were chosen to be the crew of the first manned Apollo mission train in the Apollo mission simulator. Left to right: *Ed White, Roger Chaffee, and Gus Grissom.*

The third stage of a Saturn 5 space vehicle is unloaded from a Super Guppy, a large cargo-carrying airplane.

New vehicles, whether intended for travel on earth or in space, are apt to need adjustments before they work properly, and the Apollo spacecraft was no exception. It failed to pass some of its tests and, as a result, the launch date was postponed to December, then to January, 1967, and finally to February.

By early January the spacecraft for the first manned Apollo flight had been moved to Pad 34 and placed atop a Saturn 1B booster rocket for its final

tests. One of these, called a "plugs-out" test, was scheduled for January 27. It would include the systems used during the countdown, the launch, and the first three hours of flight. During the test the spacecraft was to operate on its own power instead of relying on power from an outside source. Moreover, for the first time since its installation on Pad 34, the capsule was to be pressurized with pure oxygen just as it would be during a space flight.

Each team of astronauts helps check

out the capsule assigned to its mission. Astronauts Grissom, White, and Chaffee had already spent many hours in their capsule. On January 27 they were on hand for the plugs-out test.

When the astronauts entered the spacecraft's command module shortly after 1 P.M., they wore silvery nylon pressure suits and bubble helmets. They strapped themselves to their couches— Grissom, the mission commander, on the left, White in the center, and Chaffee on the right. The couches were surrounded by switches, dials, and indicators. Multi-colored cables wound around the spacecraft's floor and disappeared into its walls.

Hooking up their pressure suits to the spacecraft's environmental control system which would supply the suits with oxygen, the three men began a preliminary check of the instruments in the cockpit. At 2:50 P.M. they were ready for the closing of the command module's airtight, double-door hatch. The cabin was then pressurized with pure oxygen at 16 pounds per square inch. (Sea level pressure is 14.7 pounds.) Radio and closed circuit television connected the astronauts, in their sealed capsule, with technicians in Pad 34's launch control center. The control center, usually referred to as the blockhouse, is located about a thousand feet from the pad.

The simulated countdown had reached T minus 10 minutes (10 minutes to blast-off) and the spacecraft was about to switch to its own power system just as it would during a real launch. Communications with the blockhouse were bad, however. The countdown was stopped while technicians located the trouble and corrected it.

It was fifteen minutes later, at 6:31 P.M., just before the count was to resume, that an anguished cry came from the spacecraft: "Fire!" It was followed a split second later by: "We've got a fire in the cockpit!" At the same moment the TV monitor in the blockhouse showed an eruption of flame, and technicians at Pad 34 noticed fire and smoke coming from the spacecraft.

During the plugs-out test, the Saturn rocket and the Apollo capsule had remained enclosed in a 310-foot-high steel gantry, a service tower used by the men working on the booster and the spacecraft. Several technicians were near the level where the capsule's hatch was located. They rushed to the hatch only to be driven back by smoke and intense heat. It was five minutes before the ground crew could open the hatch.

Inside the flame-filled capsule the three astronauts had died within seconds. They had no chance to escape.

The Apollo spacecraft did have a launch escape system, a 33-foot-high, rocket-powered tower that sat atop the capsule. In case of trouble during launch or immediately afterward, the escape system was designed to pull the capsule away from the booster and carry it to an altitude from which it could descend safely by parachute. But on January 27 the spacecraft was still enclosed in its steel gantry. Moreover, the fire was burning inside the capsule itself; separating the capsule from the Saturn booster would have done no good.

As part of their training, the astronauts had learned to leave the Apollo capsule in 90 seconds. To do this, Astronaut White, whose couch was closest to the hatch, had to turn six bolts with a torque wrench to open the inner hatch. A quick-release mechanism opened the outer hatch. During the 90 seconds, the astronauts had to unstrap themselves from their couches, unplug oxygen lines, and disconnect radio wires prior to sliding backward through the open hatch. Instead of the necessary 90 seconds, Astronauts Grissom, White, and Chaffee probably had less than 15 seconds. It wasn't enough.

The plugs-out test on Pad 34 had been considered non-hazardous. There was no fuel in the Saturn rocket and none in the spacecraft. What had gone wrong? An accident review board was appointed to find the answer. Meanwhile, the nation mourned the loss of three astronauts who might someday have gone to the moon.

After studying the construction of the Apollo capsule, examining the charred spacecraft, interviewing hundreds of technicians, and reviewing the records of the plugs-out test, the board reported its findings. Sparks from faulty wiring had ignited flammable material in the cockpit and the flame, fed by the 100 per cent oxygen inside the capsule, had spread too quickly for the astronauts to escape.

Although the condition of the burned spacecraft made it impossible to locate the exact point where the fire began, the board theorized that it was somewhere under Astronaut Grissom's couch on the left-hand side of the cabin. Wires in that area may have been frayed by the opening and closing of a small door. The resulting spark ignited Velcro strips, the sticky material that was

Members of the accident review board examine components from the Apollo spacecraft that burned on Pad 34.

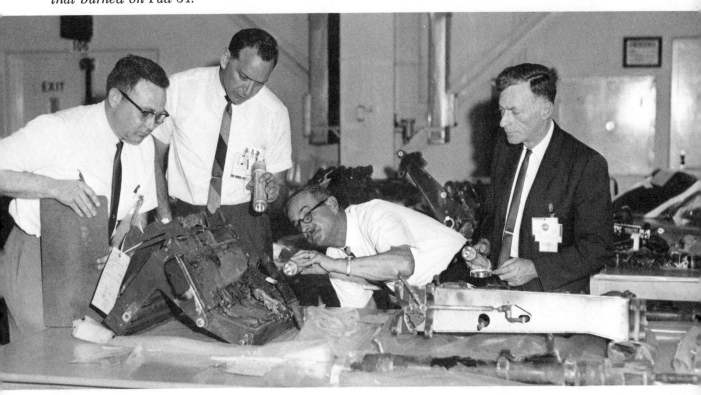

It is most likely that the fire began in this severely damaged area.

distributed along the cabin walls to hold small objects when they weren't in use. The burning Velcro, in turn, ignited nylon nets which covered the walls of the spacecraft to prevent articles from falling into equipment areas during testing. By the time the astronauts, encased in pressure suits and helmets, noticed the fire, it was already spreading rapidly.

Within 15 seconds heat from the blaze raised the pressure inside the capsule to at least 29 pounds per square inch, enough to rupture the cabin floor. Flames rushed toward the opening. The cabin filled with smoke and carbon dioxide which got into the astronauts' breathing apparatus and asphyxiated them.

According to the review board, a number of deficiencies had contributed to the fatal Apollo fire. The capsule's wiring was unsatisfactory and there were other defects in the design and workmanship of the spacecraft. In the cabin were many flammable materials, and the use of pure oxygen to pressurize the capsule added greatly to the fire hazard. Above all, as the board pointed

Women working on Beta cloth for the redesigned Apollo spacesuits.

out, no adequate provision had been made to rescue the astronauts from a potentially dangerous situation.

Even before the board submitted its report, Space Administration officials began a review of the Apollo program. Within a year they had made more than 1,500 changes inside the spacecraft. Wiring was rearranged and insulated. A less flammable, but equally sticky, Velcro replaced the kind that had been used before. The astronauts' couches were covered with a glass-fiber fabric called Beta cloth. Beta cloth, which does not burn, can withstand temperatures up to 1,500 degrees. The same material was also used in new pressure suits for the astronauts.

Using nonflammable materials such as Beta cloth greatly reduced the risk of fire. Adding nitrogen to the spacecraft's all-oxygen atmosphere would also reduce the fire risk. But on the latter point there was a disagreement. Although the air we breathe contains both nitrogen and oxygen as well as traces of other gases, Projects Mercury and Gemini had demonstrated that astronauts can work well in an all-oxygen atmosphere. An all-oxygen system has the undeniable advantage of being light, and it is easy to use. To add nitrogen would create problems of storage, mixing, and delivery. Moreover, if a spacecraft containing nitrogen in its atmosphere should experience a sudden decompression, the nitrogen in the astronauts' blood would fizz like soda pop. This painful and sometimes fatal condition, called the bends, troubles deep-sea divers who rise to the surface too rapidly.

But pure oxygen in a spacecraft is a definite fire hazard. When a substance burns, it combines with oxygen—the more oxygen, the faster the burning.

After weighing the arguments for and against continuing to use pure oxygen in the Apollo capsule, NASA decided on a compromise. When a space capsule was on the launching pad and its interior pressure had to be high, it would be filled with a mixture of 60 per cent oxygen and 40 per cent nitrogen. (In the atmosphere the mixture is roughly 21 per cent oxygen and 78 per cent nitrogen.) The astronauts would continue to have pure oxygen pumped into their space suits, however. After the capsule left the earth's atmosphere, its cabin would be flooded with pure oxygen, but only a relatively safe five pounds of pressure per square inch would be needed in space.

NASA's decision pleased the astronauts. They wanted to be able to take off their pressure suits during long journeys. With pure oxygen in the capsule they wouldn't have to worry about getting the bends when they went outside the capsule for EVA (extravehicular activity) assignments.

The astronauts were also pleased with

To open the Apollo capsule's new quick-escape hatch, astronauts pump a handle back and forth.

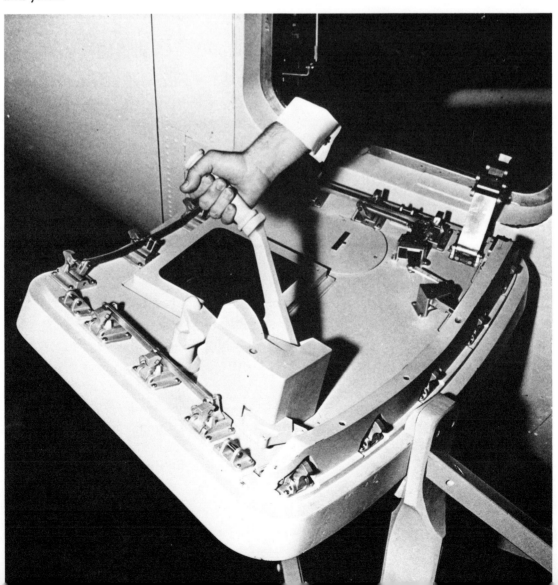

the Apollo capsule's new quick-escape hatch door. It opened in less than three seconds and three astronauts could leave the capsule in less than 17 seconds.

As the Space Administration prepared to resume the Apollo program, its goal remained the same: astronauts on the moon before 1970. But now there was real doubt about whether that goal could be reached. Moreover, in the aftermath of the tragic fire, some Americans wondered not only if the goal could be reached, but also if the nation should continue to strive toward it.

"Is going to the moon worth what it costs?" the critics asked. They pointed out that Project Apollo was costing billions of dollars. In addition, the space program was tying up a large share of the nation's scientific talent.

Other critics were in favor of the United States' sending astronauts to the moon, but they pointed to the fire as evidence that Project Apollo was trying to do too much too soon. "Why does a lunar landing have to be made by 1970?" they argued. "Why not proceed more slowly and make sure it can be done safely?"

Space officials acknowleged that the fire on Pad 34 had taught them some hard lessons about building and launching spacecraft. "Fire is something which we will never underestimate again," said Dr. Kurt H. Debus, director of NASA's Kennedy Space Center. But there could be another accident. "We cannot eliminate all the risks," acknowledged Cape Kennedy's safety director. "Risk is the name of the game."

And Astronauts Grissom, White, and Chaffee would have agreed. Veteran spaceman Grissom had spoken for them all when he had said: "If we die, we want people to accept it. The conquest of space is worth the risk of life."

Back Into Space

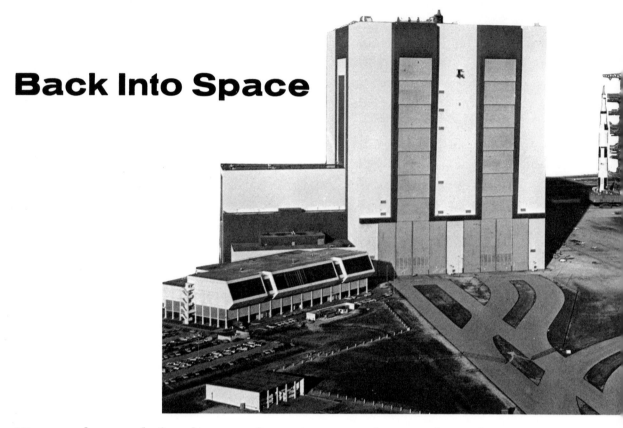

Nine months passed after the tragic fire on Pad 34 before NASA attempted another Apollo launching. It was an unmanned test, but a very important one because the giant Saturn 5 rocket was to travel into space for the first time. The Saturn would not leave from Pad 34, however, because Pad 34 was much too small for the big rocket. The crucial test, aptly called "Big Shot," required the use of the Space Administration's huge new launching facilities at the John F. Kennedy Space Center on Merritt Island, adjacent to Cape Kennedy.

At the Kennedy Space Center everything is big, but the biggest structure of all is the Vehicle Assembly Building (VAB) where the three stages of the

Saturn are first joined together and then to the spacecraft. The VAB is 52 stories high, 710 feet long, and 515 feet wide—one of the largest buildings in the world in terms of volume. If the VAB's air conditioning system were to fail, clouds would form inside the huge structure, and rain would fall.

The first stage of the test Saturn arrived at the moonport by barge from NASA's Mississippi Test Facility on the Gulf of Mexico. Another barge carried the second stage from California by way of the Panama Canal. These stages were too large to be moved by any other means, but the smaller third stage arrived at the Space Center in a Super Guppy cargo plane. The three stages

Upper left: *Perched atop a crawler-transporter, the assembled Apollo-Saturn 5 space vehicle and its mobile launcher leave the VAB for the launch site.*

Above: *Inside the Vehicle Assembly Building an Apollo spacecraft is mated with a Saturn 5 rocket. The spacecraft consists of the cone-shaped command module (at the top); the cylindrical service module; and the adaptor, with the lunar module (not visible) inside.*

were assembled on a mobile launcher in one of the VAB's four immense bays.

The launcher alone weighed 5,750 tons.

After an Apollo spacecraft had been lifted into place atop the Saturn, a huge vehicle called a crawler-transporter moved under the mobile launcher and carried the whole assembly from the VAB to Launch Pad 39A, three and a half miles away. The trip took about seven hours. The crawler-transporter traveled on four double tracks on a road as wide as an eight-lane highway. The road was made of crushed rock, one of the few substances that could bear such a heavy load. After depositing the mobile launcher with its Saturn and space-

craft on the pad, the crawler-transporter returned to the VAB for the mobile service structure that would be used during the launch preparations.

Originally scheduled for September, the Saturn test had to be postponed because of trouble in the rocket's second-stage engine. On November 9, 1967, however, the mission was ready to go. Excitement was high at the Kennedy Space Center. Saturn 5 was the rocket that would send men to the moon. It was also the first time any rocket had been launched from the new moonport.

Wernher von Braun, whose Marshall Space Flight Center was largely responsible for the development of the Saturn, was among the thousands who traveled

NASA's huge crawler-transporter has to carry a load of 12 million pounds—the combined weight of a fully loaded Apollo-Saturn 5 space vehicle and its mobile launcher. Each of the 60 steel links in the crawler-transporter's tread weighs about a ton.

to Florida to watch the important launching. "The first launching of a new and untested rocket is the acid test of the work performed for years and years preceding the launch," von Braun said. "We are confident that this rocket is well designed, that it is well built and that, once it is safely off the pad, it will fly well."

Von Braun's confidence was justified. Carrying an unmanned Apollo capsule, the mighty Saturn roared from Launch Pad 39A exactly on time. Although the rocket's third stage had been tested as part of a Saturn 1B booster, its first two stages had never flown before. All three stages performed flawlessly.

Within minutes after blast-off, the Apollo spacecraft and the Saturn third stage were in an orbit 115 miles above the earth. After two orbits, the third-stage engine successfully re-ignited to send the spacecraft 10,000 miles from the earth. The spacecraft's own SPS engine increased its distance from the earth to 11,234 miles and then sent it plunging back into the atmosphere at a speed that reached 25,000 miles an hour. The capsule landed safely in the Pacific Ocean about 600 miles northwest of Hawaii after eight hours and 37 minutes in space.

During the flight, designated Apollo 4, NASA had attempted to test both the spacecraft's and the rocket's systems, and the "all up" testing had been a tremendous success, saving both time and

Shortly before blast-off, the mobile service structure used during launch preparations at the Kennedy Space Center is rolled away from the launch pad.

money. Space officials were jubilant. Wernher von Braun called it "the greatest day of my life." Beyond any doubt, Project Apollo had taken a big step toward a landing on the moon.

Only one key element of the Apollo moon program was still untested. This was the lunar module in which two astronauts would travel to the moon's surface. Like the Apollo spacecraft, the LM had been remodeled after the fatal fire to make it safer. As a result, it was January 22, 1968, before the craft was ready to fly in space for the first time. It was not going to the moon. Instead, the LM would be carried into orbit on the nose of a Saturn 1B booster and its ascent and descent engines would be tested one hundred miles above the earth.

With a computer-directed robot that space technicians called the "mechanical boy" at the controls, the lunar module successfully separated from the Saturn and started up its own 10,000-pound-thrust descent engine. This was the engine that would brake the LM to a gentle lunar touchdown. Instead of burning for the required 39 seconds, however, the engine shut down after only four seconds.

At NASA's Manned Spacecraft Center engineers were monitoring the LM's flight. When they discovered that an on-board computer had shut the engine down because thrust did not build up fast enough, they quickly bypassed the computer and successfully fired the descent engine two times. Then they started up the ascent engine that would carry astronauts away from the moon. As the engine fired, the two sections of the LM snapped apart as they would during a lunar mission and the ascent section soared away from the descent section. Later, the engine was fired a second time to end the Apollo 5 test. According to NASA's Associate Administrator for Manned Space Flight, George Mueller, the LM had made "an excellent flight."

NASA was almost ready to send the first Apollo astronauts into space. First, however, the Saturn 5 and the Apollo capsule had to be tested one more time.

Apollo 6's countdown on April 4, 1968, was flawless. The giant Saturn 5 lifted into the morning sky with a roar that rattled windows for miles around. But trouble was only minutes away. When the Saturn's second-stage engines took over, two of them burned for only four minutes instead of the required six. This upset the remainder of the flight plan. And that was not the only trouble in store for Apollo 6.

Three hours after launch, the Apollo 6 spacecraft and the third stage of the Saturn rocket were in an earth orbit. The third-stage engine was supposed to boost the capsule out of the orbit but it refused to re-ignite. "We didn't even get a burp out of it," said one engineer.

This was a serious failure. If Apollo 6 had been a manned mission, the astronauts in the spaceship would have

High over the Atlantic Ocean, the first stage of Apollo 6's Saturn 5 rocket separates from the second stage. In the background is the earth.

abandoned all hope of going to the moon and would have immediately returned to earth, using the craft's SPS engine to bring it out of orbit. Since Apollo 6 was unmanned, flight controllers separated the spacecraft from the third stage. Because they wanted to bring Apollo 6 down from a great height to test its heat shield, they directed the spacecraft's SPS engine to send it 13,821 miles into space. From that height it hurtled back into the atmosphere. The spacecraft landed 250 miles short of its target area in the Pacific.

Apollo 6 was less than a perfect mission. At first space officials feared that they would have to send up another unmanned test—at a cost of $200 million and valuable time—before proceeding with manned flight. But the Saturn's trouble proved to be minor. A fuel-line leak and a pair of crossed wires had caused the second-stage engine to shut down. A fuel-line leak had also been responsible for the failure of the third-stage engine to restart. These defects could be corrected without another test flight and NASA announced that Apollo 7, the first manned Apollo mission, would be the next to leave the launching pad. Its booster would be the smaller Saturn 1B rocket.

Apollo 7 was planned as the first of a series of manned flights, each one taking Apollo a step closer to a landing on the moon. The primary objective of the pioneer manned flight was to prove that the 16-ton moonship was spaceworthy and ready for the 500,000-mile round trip to the moon. The testing was to be done during an earth orbiting mission that might continue as long as 11 days. If Apollo 7 had to be brought down sooner

than that, the flight would still be worthwhile because the most important maneuvers were planned for early in the mission.

One space veteran, Navy Captain Walter M. Schirra, and two rookies, Air Force Major Donn F. Eisele, and Walter Cunningham, a scientist-astronaut, made up the Apollo 7 crew. Schirra, the spacecraft commander and one of the original Mercury astronauts, had flown both Mercury and Gemini missions. His two crewmen were undaunted by their first space trip. "I'm not nervous at all," said Donn Eisele. "I'm looking forward to it very eagerly. We've been working on it

A connecting section between the first and second stages of the Saturn 5 rocket falls away after the stages have separated.

This photograph was taken by the Apollo 7 astronauts as they approached the separated second stage of the Saturn 1B rocket during their simulated docking maneuver high over the Mississippi Gulf Coast. The round, white disc inside the open panels of the second stage is a docking target similar to the one used on lunar modules during moon missions.

so long, and now that it's finally at hand, we want to get on with it."

The Apollo 7 astronauts were to fly essentially the same mission that had been assigned to Astronauts Virgil Grissom, Edward White, and Roger Chaffee. Since the fire on Pad 34, NASA had spent more than $110 million in an attempt to ensure that such a tragedy did not happen again. As a result, Astronauts Schirra, Eisele, and Cunningham climbed into a vastly improved spacecraft on the morning of October 11, 1968. In addition, new safety measures were in effect on Pad 34 to speed up escape in case trouble did develop before blast-off.

Although NASA was confident that everything possible had been done to insure the success of Apollo 7, there was more than the usual amount of tension as the countdown progressed on Pad 34. It was the first manned launch since three astronauts had been killed on that same pad. And it was the first time astronauts had attempted to take an Apollo capsule into space. If a major problem developed, it would all but wipe out any hope of landing Americans on the moon before 1970.

When Apollo 7 left Pad 34 atop a flame-spouting Saturn 1B rocket at 10:03 A.M., a concerned nation followed its progress on television. A remarkable

70

camera called IGOR (for Intercept Ground Optical Recorder) photographed Apollo 7 until it was more than 100 miles away. TV viewers saw the Saturn's first stage shut down and separate and the second stage ignite. They also saw the tall escape tower rocket away from the spacecraft when it was no longer needed.

From inside the Apollo spacecraft Astronaut Schirra saw the tower leave, too. "Oh, beautiful. The tower really jettisoned," he said.

Ten and a half minutes after launch, out of IGOR's range, Apollo 7 went into an orbit that varied from 141 to 176 miles above the earth. "It sure is a fantastic world up here," reported veteran spaceman Walter Schirra.

Back on the ground there was momentary confusion at the Houston Manned Spacecraft Center when an electrical failure darkened the consoles that were monitoring the flight. The Center's busy computers were unaffected, however, and power was restored after a few minutes. So far all of Apollo 7's problems seemed to be on the ground.

"This is fine," Astronaut Schirra radioed from more than a hundred miles above the earth. "We're having a ball."

Apollo 7 had gone into orbit still attached to the Saturn 1B's second stage. At the end of the first orbit, the Saturn was actuated by radio to dump all of its remaining fuel. Then Mission Commander Schirra separated the spacecraft from the second stage. Instead of moving away from the Saturn, however, he maneuvered close to it. This was a rehearsal for a moon mission when the command module would have to dock with a lunar module carried at the top of a Saturn 5's third stage. Apollo 7 did not dock because the Saturn 1B carried no LM. Instead, Schirra simulated the docking maneuver by coming to within five feet of the Saturn. After the simulated docking, the Apollo astronauts fired the spacecraft's thrusters to drop their capsule into an orbit lower than the Saturn's.

Astronaut Schirra began his second day in orbit with a head cold, the first time that this had happened to an American astronaut during a space mission. The Apollo crew was prepared for just such an emergency. Their medical supplies included aspirin and decongestant tablets, and Schirra took some of both. He reported that his temperature was normal.

"I haven't been coughing," Schirra told the flight surgeon on duty at the Manned Spacecraft Center. "There's nothing in the lungs."

In spite of his cold, Schirra was at the controls when Apollo 7 rendezvoused with the orbiting Saturn second stage, which had moved away from the spacecraft during the night. A ten-second burn of the spacecraft's SPS engine began the 3½-hour chase. Using Apollo's sextant and telescope-like sighting device for guidance, the astronauts closed in on the Saturn from 80 miles behind it. After one more burn of the SPS engine, and some maneuvering with the spacecraft's thrusters, Apollo 7 was only 70 feet from the Saturn. Because the rocket was tumbling wildly, that was as close as the astronauts wanted to get. After 20 minutes the spacecraft moved away. The rocket would continue to orbit for a few more days and then burn up when it re-entered the earth's atmosphere.

"We were nominal," Schirra informed Mission Control at the end of the exercise. Nominal is a term spacemen use to mean "just as planned."

Mission Control congratulated the Apollo crew on the skillful rendezvous. "Thank you," replied Schirra. "We're accepting some of that today. It was a real job."

Apollo 7 had successfully accomplished a maneuver that might someday rescue astronauts stranded in lunar orbit. Moreover, the Apollo 7 crew had completed the rendezvous visually, guided by data from their own small computer. The big computers at Mission Control had supplied information for the initial orbit changes.

As they traveled around the earth, the three spacemen took photographs of the ground beneath them, tracked the orbiting Saturn from as far as 320 miles away, and dealt with several small problems that developed in the spacecraft. They also registered a complaint with Mission Control. "I feel, at least, that we're getting more food than we need and Wally feels the same way," Astronaut Cunningham radioed. "Donn seems to be eating most of his, though. Probably in a couple of days, I will skip a whole meal."

On the subject of exercise in space Cunningham reported: "You start noticing that your lower abdominal muscles seem a little sore. You float around in a seated position and they kind of bunch up. After the exerciser you feel much better." He was referring to the stretchable cords that the astronauts pulled to keep their muscles in shape.

Astronaut Schirra was still bothered by his cold, and his traveling companions thought they might be catching colds too. Perhaps because of the colds, the space travelers complained about not getting enough sleep. They found the bag-like sleeping hammocks suspended beneath the left and right couches warm and uncomfortable and preferred to remain in the couches. There, however, they were bothered by light flooding through the spacecraft windows.

After the first hours of flight, the astronauts had removed their bulky pressure suits. Walter Schirra and Donn Eisele replaced the suits with the Apollo in-flight coveralls. The blue two-piece coveralls had several pockets in which the astronauts could store small articles. Each man wore a lightweight headset with the coveralls.

Astronaut Cunningham reported that he felt more comfortable in just the constant-wear garment designed to be worn under both the pressure suit and the in-flight coveralls. It was a porous-knit cotton suit that resembled long underwear.

On October 14 Apollo 7 turned on its TV camera and 15 million Americans watched a smiling trio of astronauts at work. The presentation was the first from American astronauts in space. At first the Apollo crew had been reluctant to make room for a TV camera in their already crowded cabin. Moreover, they thought that they had enough to do without spending time on TV programs. A presentation scheduled for October 12 did have to be canceled because the astronauts were too busy rendezvousing with the Saturn rocket to get the camera ready. Since then they had found time

Smiling Apollo 7 astronauts display a message for their audience during the first television transmission from American astronauts in space.

to prepare a sign which they held in front of the camera at the beginning of the telecast. It read: "Hello from the lovely Apollo room high atop of everything."

Only two ground stations, one at Cape Kennedy and another at Corpus Christi, Texas, were equipped to receive TV signals from Apollo 7. They converted the 10-frames-per-second pictures to 30-frames-per-second and relayed them to Mission Control in Houston from where they were sent to the TV networks. Because its TV signals could be received only as it sped across the southern part of the United States, Apollo 7's programs lasted from 7 to 11 minutes. That was long enough for the astronauts to transmit surprisingly clear pictures of themselves and their capsule. They also trained the TV camera on spacecraft windows to give viewers glimpses of the earth.

Apollo 7 reached the halfway point in its trail-blazing journey with nearly three quarters of its assignments completed. It had been 128 hours in space, had covered two million miles, and had completed 82 orbits of the earth. It had achieved 24 of 36 primary flight objectives and 12 of 15 secondary objectives.

"The flight continues to go very smoothly," reported Apollo 7 Flight Director Glynn Lunney. "So smoothly, in fact, that the crew has even stopped complaining about their head colds."

While the astronauts were traveling around the earth, Hurricane Gladys moved into the Gulf of Mexico. On its ninety-first orbit, Apollo 7 passed directly over the storm.

"Man, that's really a spinner," reported Walter Schirra.

Schirra and Cunningham moved as

73

Astronaut Cunningham uses a special space pen for writing during the Apollo 7 flight. Note the film magazine floating above his hand in the weightless environment of the spacecraft.

fast as they could from one of the spacecraft's windows to another, trying to get good photos of the swirling hurricane. "We looked like squirrels in a cage," the mission commander observed later. The astronauts described the eye of the storm as "a little depressed dimple" in the center of a mass of clouds. Their description of the hurricane and information on its location were relayed to the National Hurricane Center in Miami, Florida.

Splashdown for Apollo 7 was scheduled for the morning of October 22. Except for a power failure early in the flight, quickly corrected by Walter Cun-

ningham, the astronauts had encountered no potentially serious problems during their long journey. The flight had included seven successful firings of the spacecraft's SPS engine to change the capsule's orbit. Moreover, one of the burns had lasted 66 seconds, the most powerful maneuver yet undertaken by American astronauts in space.

Bringing a spacecraft back to earth is a dangerous and difficult procedure. For Apollo 7 it threatened to be even more dangerous than usual because the astronauts had not recovered from their colds. If their sinuses had become blocked, the increase in pressure as the capsule re-entered the earth's atmosphere might rupture their eardrums. At the very least they would experience severe pain.

To help unblock their stuffed-up heads, the astronauts took three doses of a decongestant. During re-entry they also planned to valsalva—that is, hold their noses shut, close their mouths, and blow hard. This would help equalize the pressure against their ears.

Mercury and Gemini astronauts had worn their helmets during re-entry to protect their heads from accidental bumps. If the Apollo 7 crew wore hel-mets, however, they would have trouble holding their noses. The ground controllers wanted the helmets on but suggested that they not be fastened to the pressure suits. Mission Commander Schirra favored leaving the helmets off altogether. This was one of several disagreements between the men on the ground and the men in space during the Apollo 7 flight. The astronauts had objected to several tests that ground controllers asked them to make. The additional tasks were not in the flight plan and the astronauts doubted their value. The Apollo crew resolved the

This photograph of Hurricane Gladys was taken from the Apollo 7 spacecraft at an altitude of 97 nautical miles.

After landing in the Atlantic, the Apollo 7 command module turned upside down. The balloon-like bags attached to the top then inflated to bring the module rightside up again.

disagreement about the helmets by coming down without them.

Early in the morning of October 22, the Apollo crew fired the spacecraft's SPS engine for the last time. The ten-second blast slowed the capsule and started it on its downward path toward the earth. Then the astronauts separated the command module from the service module that contained the SPS engine. Inside the command module the astro-

nauts were strapped to their couches, braced for the shock of hitting the earth's atmosphere and a landing in the Atlantic Ocean. Apollo 7 splashed down at 6:12 A.M. about a thousand miles east of Cape Kennedy.

Apollo 7 ended its successful journey upside down and it remained upside down for several minutes. During that time recovery helicopters from the carrier *Essex* could not hear the capsule's

On board the U.S.S. Essex, NASA officials examine the Apollo 7 command module.

rescue beacon. When the balloon-like bags that were part of the spacecraft's equipment inflated to right it, the helicopters homed in on the beacon. Within minutes the three astronauts were on the flight deck of the *Essex*. They were slightly wobbly from 11 days in a weightless condition, but their ears were apparently unharmed.

"It's great to be back," said Schirra. "The mission went beautifully."

During 260 hours and 10 minutes of space flight, Astronauts Walter Schirra, Donn Eisele, and Walter Cunningham traveled 4.5 million miles in 163 trips around the earth. They had proved that the Apollo capsule could remain in space long enough and function well enough to take men to the moon. The success of Apollo 7 had paved the way for the trail-blazing lunar journey of Apollo 8.

Spider and Gumdrop

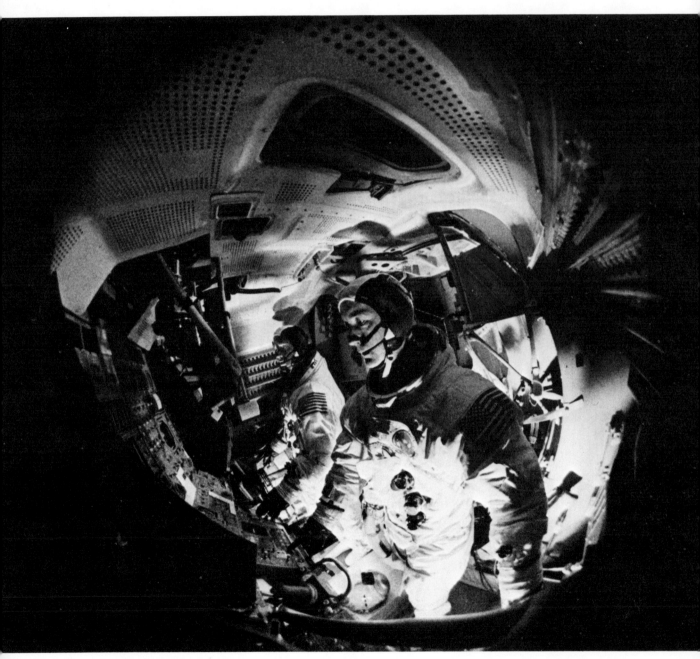

Standing at the controls of the lunar module simulator, Astronauts McDivitt and Schweickart practice the maneuvers they will use when they test the LM during the Apollo 9 flight.

During their earth-orbiting flight in Apollo 7, Astronauts Schirra, Eisele, and Cunningham demonstrated that NASA and its suppliers had developed an excellent spacecraft.

Astronauts Borman, Lovell, and Anders in the Christmas flight of Apollo 8 proved that the spacecraft could fly to the moon, orbit it, and return safely.

The next step toward attaining the nation's space goal was a manned test of the lunar module—the vehicle that would make the actual landing on the moon. So far, the LM had had one unmanned flight in space—during the Apollo 5 mission. NASA, therefore, planned Apollo 9 as a first manned test of the LM. It was an important, but dangerous, test. If the LM's engines malfunctioned in space, it might be impossible to rescue the two astronauts conducting the test.

For Apollo 9, which one space official described as "the toughest United States manned space mission yet," NASA chose Air Force Colonel James McDivitt, a veteran of a 66-orbit voyage in Gemini 4; Air Force Colonel David Scott, who had flown in Gemini 8; and Russell Schweickart, a civilian astronaut who was making his first trip into space. During Apollo 9's fifth day in earth orbit, Mission Commander McDivitt and Lunar Module Pilot Schweickart were going to fly the LM 100 miles away from the Apollo 9 spacecraft and then fly back again. While they were in the LM, Command Module Pilot Scott would be handling the three-man Apollo capsule alone.

In a preflight interview Colonel McDivitt explained the mission. "The purpose of this flight," he said, "is to find out what's wrong with the LM, so we can fix it. I'd be surprised if we find something to spoil the mission, but I'm sure something is going to fail. You just can't launch something this complex without something failing."

Apollo 9 was originally scheduled for February 28, 1969. On that day the spacecraft and a giant Saturn 5 booster were checked out and ready to go, but all three astronauts had developed stuffy noses and sore throats. Dr. Berry, the astronauts' physician, recommended that the flight be delayed. "The only thing I could guarantee is that we would have three sick crewmen if we launched Friday," Dr. Berry said.

In an orbiting spacecraft, a hearty sneeze could fill the cabin with a thousand floating droplets. If an astronaut felt ill, he might make a mistake during an important maneuver. And if he should throw up while wearing his helmet, he could choke to death.

By March 3 the astronauts were feeling much better. Dr. Berry declared them "healthy and ready" for the launch which was scheduled for 11 A.M. "I think the chances of recurrence in flight are exceedingly slim," the doctor told newsmen.

The countdown for Apollo 9 was a smooth one. A mission commentator in Pad 39A's blockhouse described the final seconds: "T minus 55 seconds and counting. All going well. We are coming up on the power transfer. Mark 50 seconds and counting. We're now on internal power with the three stages and instrument unit of the Saturn 5. All propellant tanks in the second stage now pressurized. Thirty-five seconds and counting, the vehicle now completely pressurized, the vents closed. We are go. Thirty seconds and counting. T minus 25 seconds and counting, all aspects still go at this time as the computer monitors. Twenty seconds, guidance release, 15, 14, 13, 12, 11, 10, 9. We have ignition sequence start, 6, 5, 4, 3, 2, 1, zero. All engines running. Commit, lift off! We have lift-off at 11 A.M.!"

According to space doctors, during the launching Astronaut McDivitt's heart rate rose from its normal 70-to-80 beats a minute to a rapid 135. Scott's increased from the 65-to-75 range to 120. But space rookie Schweickart's rate went only to 72 from its normal range in the mid-60s. With the exception of Schweickart's, the increases were as expected. However, Schweickart, who was subject to airsickness, had taken an anti-nausea pill and that may have affected his heart rate.

A few minutes after launch when Apollo 9's Saturn booster had jettisoned its first stage and the launch escape tower had rocketed away from the spacecraft, the three astronauts received a cheerful message from the ground: "Apollo 9, you are go all the way. Everything looks good."

Unfortunately, that report soon changed. When Apollo 9 went into orbit, its on-board computer showed a flight path that ranged from 102 to 188 miles above the earth. At the same time, computers on the ground indicated that Apollo 9 was in a 118-mile-high circular orbit. If the spacecraft's computer was not working properly, the mission might have to be terminated. Investigation proved that the on-board computer was not at fault. Instead, the process of feeding information into it needed ad-

justment. A few hours later the Manned Spacecraft Center at Houston was able to report: "The computer is go at this time."

Early in their first orbit the Apollo 9 crew began an important maneuver, one that had never been attempted in space before. They were going to dock their command module with the lunar module housed in the adaptor section at the tip of the Saturn's third stage. The third stage had shut down after boosting Apollo 9 into orbit, but it was still attached to the spacecraft.

Command Module Pilot Scott started the docking maneuver by firing explosive bolts to separate the capsule from the Saturn third stage. He then fired the spacecraft's thrusters to move it 50 feet away from the third stage. As Apollo 9 left the Saturn, the adaptor at the rocket's forward end opened to reveal the LM.

Using the spacecraft's thrusters again, Scott turned it around to face the LM. The astronauts reported their progress to Mission Control: "It's out there and we're turned around and proceeding with the station keeping and docking." While station keeping, they would fly close to the third stage to examine the LM. When they docked, they would actually link up with the LM.

Approximately half an hour later another message came from Apollo 9: "All right, Houston, we're hard docked." Apollo 9 had inserted its docking probe into the LM's docking collar and the two spacecraft were firmly latched together.

During docking the LM had remained attached to the Saturn. The astronauts' next task, therefore, was to separate the LM from the rocket. After pressurizing

"We are about 25 feet and are closing." Apollo 9 approaches the Saturn third stage prior to docking with the lunar module at its tip. The adaptor panels (see page 80) have been jettisoned, revealing the LM.

The 85-foot antenna near Madrid in Spain helps track spacecraft on lunar missions. There are two other such stations. One of the three always provides a communications link with the spacecraft.

the smaller vehicle from the command module's oxygen tanks, they fired explosive springs to eject the LM from the Saturn. Using the command module's thrusters, they maneuvered the combined spacecraft to a safe distance from the orbiting Saturn. Shortly afterward, ground controllers restarted the Saturn's engine to send it into a looping solar orbit.

The astronauts saw it go.

"It's just like a great star disappearing into the distance," McDivitt reported. "We've got some movies but I'm not sure they're going to be too good."

Once the Saturn third stage was safely out of the way, the busy astronauts fired their own SPS engine to put the combined spacecraft into a new orbit which ranged from 124 to 143 miles above the earth. The five-second burn produced an orbit that would last longer than the old one, and at the same time it tested the capsule's autopilot—a device that automatically keeps it on a set course. Apollo 9's orbit change was part of the crew's preparations for the crucial maneuvers that would begin the next day.

After studying the sleeping problems of the Apollo 7 and 8 crews, NASA had decided that the Apollo 9 astronauts should all sleep at the same time. While they were resting their spacecraft would be in drifting, or unguided, flight with almost all spacecraft systems turned off or down—except the environmental control system that regulated the capsule's atmosphere, temperature, and pressure.

Ten hours and 51 minutes after Apollo 9's launching, Mission Control announced that the crew had begun their first rest period. Astronaut Mc-

Divitt was in his left-hand couch, Scott in the couch on the right, and Schweickart in a hammock-like sleeping bag beneath one of the couches. McDivitt and Scott continued to wear their communications headsets, but they had turned the receiver volume down. Moreover, Mission Control planned to keep communications with the spacecraft at a minimum during the rest period.

While the astronauts slept, NASA's Manned Space-Flight Tracking Network kept a close check on the orbiting Apollo 9. Fourteen ground stations, four ships, and six airplanes made up the network. Each unit was equipped to receive voice communications and electronically transmitted data from the spacecraft for relay to the Mission Control Center at Houston. They also relayed messages to the astronauts.

Apollo's ground stations were located at Cape Kennedy; Bermuda; Grand Bahama Island; Antigua; Canary Island; Ascension Island; Madrid, Spain; Carnarvon, Australia; Honeysuckle Creek, Australia; Guam; Kokee, Hawaii; Guaymas, Mexico; Goldstone, California; and Corpus Christi, Texas. The sites at Madrid, Honeysuckle Creek, and Goldstone had huge 85-foot antennas. As Apollo 9 circled the earth, tracking responsibility was transferred from one station to another. The ships and planes filled in the gaps between the ground stations.

NASA's Manned Space-Flight Tracking Network dates back to Project Mercury. It was expanded for Project Gemini and again for Apollo until some $500 million had been invested in it. During an Apollo flight 4,000 people were on duty at the various stations.

"Good morning, Apollo 9, Houston." The call from Mission Control began the Apollo 9 astronauts' second day in space. They answered with a cheerful "Good morning, Houston. This is Apollo 9." After Mission Control reported that no problems had developed during the night, one of the still sleepy astronauts remarked: "I guess we have to wake up now, huh?"

In addition to sleeping at the same time, the Apollo 9 flight plan called for the astronauts to eat together whenever possible. Therefore, all three had breakfast before beginning the day's activities. These centered around three more firings of Apollo 9's SPS engine. The firings reduced the spacecraft's weight by using up fuel and allowed the astronauts to check its performance while docked with the LM. The three burns also changed the spacecraft's orbit to insure that it would be in daylight and within range of tracking stations when the astronauts performed critical maneuvers during the lunar module's test flight.

At the end of the day's third burn Jim McDivitt reported: "We just want to advise you that the command and service module now weighs less than the LM." The capsule communicator at

The Mercury *is one of three ships which support Apollo spacecraft during insertion into earth orbit and the start of the long trajectory to the moon.*

Houston answered: "Hey, Jim, I think you might like the heavy job. Soon as you get this one lighter, now tomorrow you are going to crawl into the heavy one." The capsule communicator was referring to the big event of Apollo 9's third day in space when Astronauts Mc-Divitt and Schweickart planned to enter the lunar module. It would be the first manning in space of the vehicle that was intended ultimately to carry astronauts to the surface of the moon.

On the big day the astronauts had been awake a little more than two hours when Mission Control radioed: "Every-thing looks good down here. You have a go for IVT [intravehicular transfer]."

The message marked the beginning of several busy hours for the Apollo 9 crew. While his teammates donned pressure suits and prepared to enter the LM, David Scott cleared the 4-foot-long, 32-inch-wide tunnel connecting the two spacecraft. He removed the command module's forward hatch and two bulky latching devices located inside the tunnel before swinging open the LM's hatch. But Scott had difficulty maneuvering the unwieldy metal pieces in the weightlessness of space and he finished an hour behind schedule.

When the tunnel was finally cleared, Astronaut Schweickart crawled into the LM headfirst. Once inside he attached a pair of rope restraints to his waist. The restraints, which were attached to the craft's walls, kept him from floating around in the LM's small cabin. Then he began to power up the LM for the day's activities.

Although Schweickart could no longer see his fellow astronauts, he was able to talk with them and with Mission Control

in Houston by radio. Soon the com-mand module received a call from the LM: "Gumdrop, Spider." Gumdrop was the command module's call sign and Spider referred to the LM.

Spider's first transmission to Gumdrop was a report on Schweickart's progress in readying the LM for occupancy. After he was joined by McDivitt, the two astronauts began a careful check of the Spider's systems which included deploying its four spindly legs.

Shortly after that maneuver, Houston received a message from Jim McDivitt in Spider: "I would like to go private with you." It was a request from the astronaut for a conversation with Mission Control that would not be auto-matically relayed to newsmen. His request was granted and he reported that Rusty Schweickart had suffered two attacks of vomiting and nausea. Schweickart had been ill before he left the command module and again after he entered the LM.

Space doctors were at a loss for an immediate explanation of Schweickart's illness. It might have been motion sick-ness, or it could have been a reaction to sleeping pills or to the anti-nausea pills Schweickart had taken. Apollo 8 Astro-naut Frank Borman thought his own illness during his moon flight was caused by sleeping pills, not intestinal flu. How-ever, Schweickart didn't think sleeping pills were responsible in his case. At any rate, he was feeling well enough to continue with the day's schedule which included a TV presentation from the LM.

For the five-minute telecast the two astronauts wore their pressure suits but not their helmets. They were standing side by side in the small, couchless LM cabin. Schweickart, as was to be expected, looked wan, but he helped McDivitt in a largely silent demonstration of the LM's interior.

After the telecast the next major item on the astronauts' flight plan was a test firing of the LM's descent engine while it was docked with the command module. "We're full throttle into the air," announced Spider when the firing began.

As the 9,870-pound-thrust engine propelled the combined craft backward through space, Spider observed: "We just threw a big hunk down on the ground there. There goes another hunk." Rapid acceleration was peeling pieces of film-like skin from the lunar module. These were only small pieces of the craft's thermal blanket and the loss posed no threat to the astronauts.

After manually taking over the controls, McDivitt shut down the LM's engine and brought the test to a close.

"That was mighty beautiful all the way," Mission Control congratulated the two astronauts.

"That's pretty smooth," agreed Dave Scott in Gumdrop.

In spite of Astronaut Schweickart's illness, the first manning of the LM in space had been a success. But Mission Control was concerned about a space walk by Schweickart planned for the next day. If he became ill again while outside the spacecraft, the results could be fatal. After McDivitt and Schweickart powered down the LM and returned to the command module, flight controllers discussed the problem with the Apollo crew. Mission Commander McDivitt recommended that the space walk

be eliminated and the EVA consist of a brief period with the LM's hatch open. His recommendation was accepted.

The decision to cut short Apollo 9's extravehicular activity did little to mar the flight since the space walk was not an important mission objective. When Astronauts McDivitt and Schweickart returned to the LM the next day, however, they decided that perhaps Apollo 9 should have a space walk after all.

McDivitt relayed the suggestion to Mission Control. He said of Schweickart: "He's feeling a lot better and he looks like—he's acting like he feels a little better. Maybe we can extend this a bit."

Mission Control agreed: "Okay, that's your judgment there, and we say go ahead if you feel that way, Jim."

In the small LM cabin McDivitt helped Schweickart prepare for his space walk. "Okay, your helmet's on and locked," he said. "Finger in the gloves. Don't need your watch, do you? Where did the checklist go? Okay, here, we don't need this thing out here."

At sunrise during Apollo 9's forty-sixth revolution of the earth, Astronaut Schweickart emerged from the LM. He was wearing his pressure suit and helmet with a gold visor to reflect sunlight. On his back he carried an 84-pound pack that served as a combination oxygen supply, communications system, and cooling unit. Astronauts would use a similar backpack when they explored the moon. A 25-foot nylon line kept him from floating too far from the spacecraft.

Schweickart left the LM feet first and moved to the craft's four-foot-long platform that the astronauts call the "front porch." There he stepped into foot restraints that looked something like a pair

Astronaut Schweickart stands on the porch of the LM while he takes photographs. On his back he carries a portable life-support system (PLSS).

Gumdrop docked with Spider (foreground). Astronaut Schweickart, on the porch of the LM, took this photograph of Astronaut Scott standing in the open hatch of the command module.

of golden slippers. As he looked at the earth 152 miles below, the astronaut, whose radio call sign became Red Rover while he was outside the spacecraft, exclaimed: "Boy, O boy, what a view!"

Both spacecraft had been depressurized to prepare for the EVA and their hatches were open. When Astronaut Scott stuck his helmeted head out of Gumdrop's hatch, McDivitt in Spider radioed the space walker: "Okay, Rusty, you can take a picture of Dave."

McDivitt and Scott were also taking pictures from their open hatches, a situation that caused Red Rover to remark: "Now we're all taking pictures of everybody else taking pictures."

During the last ten minutes of his space walk, Red Rover left the golden slippers, moved along a handrail and retrieved an experiment from the outside of the LM. The EVA was going exceptionally well and Red Rover radioed that he was "feeling fine." After consulting with McDivitt, however, Mission Control recommended that the space walker not work his way over to Gumdrop as had been originally planned. That maneuver would take more time than the astronauts could spare. Therefore, after 38 minutes out in space, Schweickart re-entered the LM.

The space walker reported that his pressure suit was very comfortable and that he had no trouble keeping his position on the outside of the LM.

When Spider and Gumdrop had been repressurized, the two astronauts in Spider presented their second telecast. During the ten-minute program they showed viewers their cabin and the docked Gumdrop as it appeared from one of the Spider's triangular windows.

"We're feeling great," they assured the audience.

That night the three spacemen, back together again in the command module, began their rest period an hour early. They wanted to be ready for the crucial test flight of the lunar module scheduled for the next day.

Ninety-two hours had passed since Apollo 9's launching when Jim McDivitt and Rusty Schweickart received the message that began their big adventure: "This is Houston. You are go for undocking." The two astronauts were in Spider and Dave Scott was alone in Gumdrop.

"We're ready." The message was from Spider to Gumdrop. Upon receiving it, Scott tripped a switch to begin the undocking maneuver. "Oh, oh," said Spider, "we didn't release."

Scott tried again. "Okay, you're free," he called. For the first time astronauts were actually flying Apollo's lunar module in space.

As the spindly-legged Spider maneuvered slowly away from Gumdrop, Scott took still and motion pictures and visually checked the gold-and-black craft. "That's a nice-looking machine," he radioed.

Spider's descent engine increased the distance between the two spacecraft to three miles. Scott could still keep an eye on the LM, however, and quickly come to its rescue if something went wrong.

One and a half orbits later McDivitt fired the Spider's engine again. "Everything looks good here," Mission Control assured the two astronauts in Spider. "It was a good burn."

McDivitt agreed, but added: "It was a little rough. It got a little rough and

"You are upside down," Gumdrop radioed when Spider, flying upside down in relation to the earth, approached the command module.

shaky . . . as I was throttling up." The astronauts were standing just a short distance above the powerful descent engine which had shaken the light-weight Spider as it fired.

Spider was now in an orbit that carried it as much as 56 miles away from Gumdrop at its farthest point. Another firing of the descent engine increased the distance even more. Shortly there-after the Spider's pilots jettisoned the descent engine and prepared to test the LM's ascent engine. It would now have to bring them back to the orbiting Gum-drop just as it would someday have to lift astronauts from the moon to a wait-ing mother ship.

Before Spider began to maneuver back toward Gumdrop, its orbit had taken it as far as 111 miles away from the larger capsule. Although Astronaut Scott in Gumdrop could no longer see Spider, he would have to find it if the ascent engine failed to start. Locating Spider would be difficult because its tracking light was out. But Scott's com-puter was keeping track of Spider's movements.

In case of serious trouble Spider would have to drift helplessly in orbit until Scott arrived to rescue the stranded astronauts. Lacking a heat shield, it could not return to earth. Neither could it remain in orbit for more than a few

Before docking with Gumdrop, Astronauts McDivitt and Schweickart photographed the orbiting command module.

days without exhausting its oxygen supply.

Like the LM's descent engine, its ascent engine performed flawlessly to start Spider on its way back to Gumdrop. Soon Spider was reporting to Mission Control: "Good friend over there in the Gumdrop can see us again."

Twice using his thrusters to correct Spider's flight path, Astronaut McDivitt flew unerringly to a rendezvous with Gumdrop. "You're the biggest, friendliest, funniest looking Spider I've ever seen," radioed Dave Scott as Spider came close.

A few minutes later Scott told Spider: "You are upside down."

McDivitt in Spider agreed, at least in part. "Yes, I was just thinking, one of us isn't rightside up," he said. One of the craft had evidently turned over in the weightlessness of space. McDivitt chose to reverse the LM.

After Scott had examined Spider and taken pictures of it, and Gumdrop had been photographed from Spider, the two craft moved together to begin the delicate docking maneuver. Astronaut Scott helped McDivitt and Schweickart zero in on Gumdrop's docking target. "You're coming fine," he said. "Just coming easy like that, looks like you are coming from an angle, but you are coming in with the right attitude. You ought to go forward and to the right a little bit."

A few seconds later Scott was able to report: "Okay, you're moving into the boundary. You're inside the capture mounting now. You're okay. Looking good." And then he called: "I have capture!"

As a buzzer signaled that the two craft were joined, McDivitt exclaimed: "Wow! I haven't heard a sound that good for a long time!"

Spider had redocked with Gumdrop. The six-hour test was over.

Since the faithful Spider could not enter the earth's atmosphere, it had to be discarded in space. McDivitt and Schweickart shut the LM down and crawled back into the command module. Shortly thereafter the two vehicles were separated and the astronauts fired the LM's ascent engine a last time to send it into a 4,600-mile-high orbit. Space officials predicted that the LM would remain in orbit more than 19 years. As it sped away, one of the astronauts remarked: "It's really moving out."

During the remainder of their ten-day flight the Apollo 9 crew continued to check the command module's systems. They also experimented with earth photography and tracking. And while they whirled around the earth, they kept an anxious eye on the weather in the Atlantic Ocean southwest of Bermuda where they were scheduled to land. From a hundred miles in space the astronauts could see whitecaps there and they were worried about landing in rough water. In fact, waves in the landing area were reported to be from six to eight feet high and swells were running to 12 feet. After studying the weather forecasts,

The crew of Apollo 9 took this view of a cyclonic storm system located about 1200 miles north of Hawaii.

Right: *Three large parachutes slow the descent of the Apollo 9 spacecraft, lowering it into the Atlantic as gently as possible.*

flight controllers decided to keep Apollo 9 in space for an extra orbit and bring it down in calmer waters east of Grand Turk Island in the Bahamas.

On March 13, after 241 hours of space flight, Apollo 9 landed safely in the Atlantic within three miles of the recovery ship U.S.S. *Guadalcanal*. The flight had successfully tested the last of the complex equipment needed to land men on the moon. With only nine months remaining before the end of the decade, the Apollo 9 astronauts had brought the United States much closer to a moon landing.

President Richard Nixon wired his congratulations to the astronauts. The telegram said: "The epic flight of Apollo 9 will be recorded in history as 10 days that thrilled the world. You have by your courage and your skill helped to shape the future of man in space."

Snoopy Scouts the Moon

*Mission Commander
Stafford and Snoopy.*

"Houston, Apollo 10. Just tried looking out as far as we could out the top hatch window. Still can't see the moon, but we'll take your word it's there." The caller was Astronaut Tom Stafford and the moon that he couldn't see was only a few hundred miles away. With his fellow Apollo 10 astronauts, John Young and Eugene Cernan, Stafford was about to go into lunar orbit. But Apollo 10's flight plan did not include a landing on the moon. That would have to wait until Apollo 11.

After the successful flight of Apollo 9, some people thought Apollo 10 should try for a lunar landing. They pointed out that all of the important parts of Project Apollo had been tested and time was running short. A more cautious view prevailed, however, because additional experience was needed, especially with navigation near the moon. When Apollo 8 flew around the moon, it had been pulled from its flight path on several occasions. Scientists suspected that the cause was dense concentrations of ma-

Astronauts Young (left) and Cernan keep fit by playing handball a few days before the launch of Apollo 10.

terial beneath the lunar surface that changed the moon's gravitational pull. The composition of the massive concentrations, called mascons, was unknown, but they could easily throw a lightweight LM off course.

Among other reasons for postponing a touchdown on the moon was the fact that the LM's landing radar had never been tested in lunar flight. And a trial run in a low lunar orbit would provide valuable information on the quantities of fuel, oxygen, water, and electrical power that would be needed for a successful landing and takeoff from the moon.

Air Force Colonel Thomas P. Stafford, Apollo 10's mission commander, Navy Commander John W. Young, the command module pilot, and Navy Commander Eugene A. Cernan, the lunar module pilot, entered their spacecraft high above the Kennedy Space Center's Launch Pad 39B on May 18, 1969. An exciting eight days lay ahead of them. The astronauts, all veterans of Gemini flights, were going to stay in lunar orbit longer than Apollo 8. And they were going to fly a lunar module to within 9.4 miles of the moon's surface.

Astronaut Stafford explained the Apollo 10 mission at a preflight news conference. "Apollo 10 is designed to tie together all the knots, to try to sort out all the unknowns and pave the way for a lunar landing mission—do everything exactly as on a landing mission except the final descent to the lunar surface," he said. "When the Apollo 11 astronauts hear our descriptions and study our photographs, we want them to feel as if they had been there themselves."

Apollo 10 followed Apollo 8's route to the moon. There was one important difference, however. This time the Apollo spacecraft was equipped with a lunar module.

After an on-time launching, Apollo 10

orbited the earth twice and completed a successful trans-lunar injection, just as Apollo 8 had done. But when they separated their capsule from the third stage of the Saturn 5 that had boosted it toward the moon, the Apollo 10 astronauts didn't move away from the rocket. Instead, they turned their spacecraft around and closed in on the lunar module sheltered in the rocket's tip. They used the same maneuvers that the Apollo 9 crew had practiced in their earth-orbit docking and they were equally skillful.

During the docking the Apollo 10 astronauts trained a new, 12-pound color TV camera on the sunlit LM. "Be docked in a second, I hope," said Astronaut Cernan as the TV picture showed the command module moving in on the lunar module.

The picture from more than 4,120 miles in space was a good one. The LM grew larger and larger as the command module approached. Viewers on earth could see its orange-colored porch and its folded legs. "Snap, snap, and we're there," Cernan announced when the docking was completed.

Apollo 10's camera was adapted from a low-light-level camera used by the armed forces. It sent back to earth black and white signals that had been passed through blue, green, and red filters. The signals were picked up by NASA's ground stations at Goldstone, California, or Honeysuckle Creek, Australia, and relayed to the Manned Spacecraft Center where technicians reprocessed the signals to produce a color image for the TV networks.

During their long coast to the moon the Apollo 10 crew encountered few problems. They didn't catch colds. And

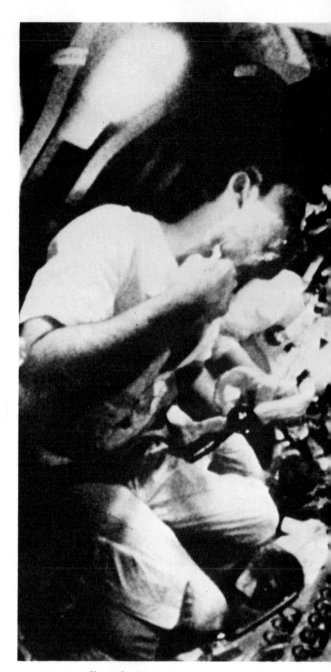

no one suffered from nausea, perhaps because Dr. Berry had recommended a series of in-flight head-movement exercises to help overcome any tendency to develop motion sickness.

Apollo 10 carried real bread into space, so the astronauts were able to make and eat sandwiches, which they did early in their flight. "We had a chicken salad sandwich," they reported to Mission Control.

96

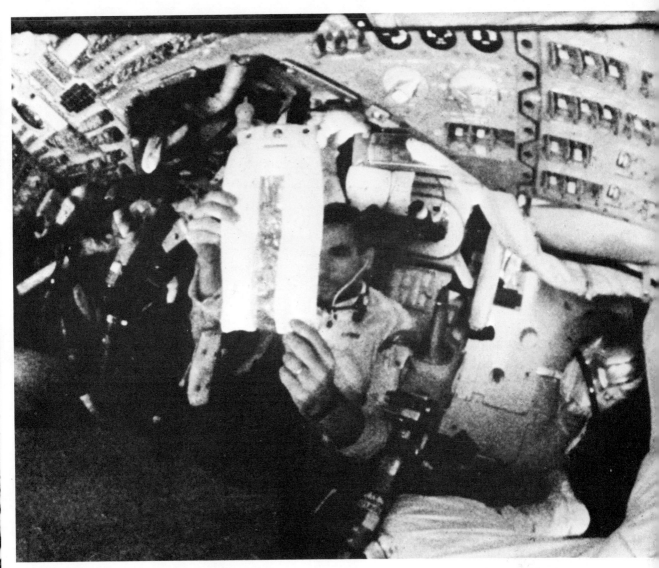

Left: *While Command Pilot Stafford looks on, Astronaut Young shaves. The Apollo 10 crew was the first to shave in space. They used brushless shaving cream that captured the shorn hair.* Above: *Astronaut Gene Cernan prepares a package of freeze-dried food.*

When asked how the sandwich tasted, they replied: "Would you believe, like a chicken salad sandwich?"

The bread they used had been flushed with nitrogen to keep it fresh. The chicken salad was a prepared spread. The spacecraft also carried ham salad spread and several "wet-pack" meals of beef and potatoes, ham and potatoes, and turkey chunks. These wet-pack meals, like Apollo 8's Christmas turkey, could be eaten with a spoon.

Although they enjoyed the sandwiches and the wet-pack meals, Stafford, Cernan, and Young were less pleased with their drinking water which became overchlorinated.

"I took a drink," reported Tom Stafford at the beginning of his second day in space, "and it was absolutely horrible."

That supply of water had to be

dumped overboard and more obtained from Apollo 10's fuel cells. The fuel cells produced water as a by-product when they generated electricity from liquid oxygen and liquid hydrogen. Apollo 10's overchlorinated water was dumped from the spacecraft through the same line that was used to dispose of urine at regular intervals during the flight. Solid body wastes were collected in bags, which were treated with a germicide and sealed before being stored in a waste disposal compartment.

Another water problem involved bubbles of hydrogen in the water that made the spacemen feel as if they had drunk too much soda pop. Because bubbles had also troubled earlier astronauts, the Apollo 10 crew had been supplied with plastic bags in which to whirl the water to remove the bubbles. Tom Stafford reported the results of the experiment to Mission Control. "What happens is that we start off with a bag full of water and bubbles—little bitty bubbles," he explained. "And we end up with a bag full of water and great big bubbles. But there is no way to separate the bubbles from the water that I can see."

The remarkably trouble-free Apollo 10 passed behind the moon after 75 hours and 48 minutes of flight. Thirty-four minutes later a message came from the spacecraft: "Houston, Apollo 10. You can tell the world that we have arrived." Apollo 10's SPS engine had put the docked command and lunar modules into orbit around the moon.

Like the Apollo 8 astronauts before them, Stafford, Cernan, and Young were anxious to describe what they saw on the lunar surface. John Young told Mission Control about an unusual feature that looked like a volcano. "It was all white on the outside, but definitely black on the top of it," he said.

When they spotted the crater Langrenus the Apollo crew radioed: "We've got Langrenus now out here off the—it depends on which way you roll—but off to the one side here. Very beautiful sharp peak right in the center."

About the moon's far side, an impressed astronaut said: "I never saw anything like that. When we came around on the back side, seems like the

This crater on the far side of the moon has central peaks and terraced sides—features which are also found in large craters on the near side of the moon.

colors are different on the back side, more—more light than they are on the front side."

The astronauts were amazed at how much they could see from a hundred miles above the lunar surface. "In earthshine you can see way down in the craters," they reported. "You can see the shadows in the craters from the earthshine, but the more you become adapted to it, it's phenomenal the amount of details you can see."

During Apollo 10's third passage be-hind the moon, a 14-second burn of its SPS engine put the spacecraft into a circular, 69-mile-high orbit which improved the moon's visibility. The astronauts had been taking still and motion pictures. Now they turned on their color TV camera and for 29 minutes showed millions of viewers the black, white, brown, and gray tones of the lunar surface. When the spacecraft passed over the area in the Sea of Tranquillity that was under consideration as the landing site for Apollo 11, they observed that it

From the command module, the Apollo 10 astronauts could see a surprising amount of detail on the lunar surface.

looked "a little bit rugged."

Apollo 10's first reports from the moon were preliminary ones because Tom Stafford and Gene Cernan planned to get a much closer look when they undocked the LM and flew it in a low lunar orbit. The astronauts began their preparations for the undocking after the TV presentation.

The Apollo 10 crew had less trouble clearing the tunnel between the command and lunar modules than the men of Apollo 9, but they encountered an unexpected problem when they removed the command module's hatch door. A rip in the door's padding had filled the tunnel with floating bits of insulation. "Hey, we're going to have a heck of a cleaning job here. They had insulation all in the seal, all in the valve, and it is really a heck of a mess up here," reported John Young, who manned the spacecraft controls while his crewmates removed some of the insulation from the tunnel.

Gene Cernan crawled through the

tunnel and entered the lunar module while Apollo 10 was behind the moon and out of contact with the earth. When communications were restored, Mission Control began to call the LM: "Snoopy, this is Houston. We're standing by. How do you read?"

During the Apollo 10 flight the LM's call sign was Snoopy and the command module was Charlie Brown. Like Snoopy, Charlie Brown's name was borrowed from a character in *Peanuts*.

Communications between Houston and the vicinity of the moon were bad, but Snoopy finally answered: "Houston, Houston, how do you read me?" Then Snoopy reported: "Everything is squared away." Lunar Module Pilot Cernan had taken care of some housekeeping chores and checked Snoopy's circuit breakers and switches. He was getting Snoopy ready for the next day when the small craft would undock from Charlie Brown and fly off on its own to orbit the moon.

"I'm personally very happy with that fellow," Cernan radioed Mission Control after he returned to the command module, "and I hope we can give you as good a report tomorrow."

When Apollo 10 began its tenth revolution of the moon after 94 hours and 29 minutes of space flight, John Young was alone in Charlie Brown. Tom Stafford and Gene Cernan were in Snoopy preparing for the most important event of the eight-day mission. If Snoopy's low-level orbit of the moon was a success, the way would be clear for Apollo 11 to land on the moon. On the other hand, if Snoopy encountered problems in undocking from Charlie Brown, during flight, or when it rejoined Charlie, Apollo 11 would have to be postponed.

"I say again, we cannot get the tunnel to vent." The message was from John Young in Charlie Brown to Mission Control. Young continued: "We've checked the in pull valve, I've checked the vent valve and Tom and Gene have checked their auto valve and their hatch seal around the hatch . . . so I don't know what the problem is. Possibly some of that insulation has gotten lodged in the vent line."

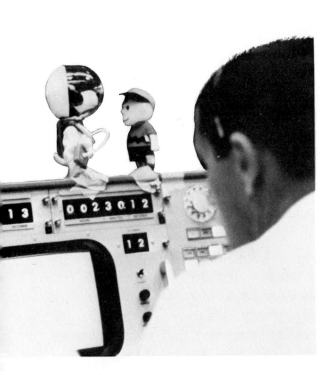

Snoopy and Charlie Brown decorate the top of a console at Mission Control Center during the Apollo 10 flight.

If the tunnel could not be vented, the extra pressure might give Snoopy an unwanted push as it undocked. However, the two astronauts in Snoopy agreed with Young that an insulation-clogged vent was probably the cause of the trouble, and they had a suggestion to make. "If we have to, we would like to go ahead and try and vent the tunnel through the LM," they radioed.

A few minutes later Stafford and Cernan reopened Snoopy's sealed hatch. Oxygen from the tunnel promptly flowed into the landing craft which had been partially depressurized. From there it was vented into space along with some of the insulation.

The tunnel pressure problem was solved, but another one took its place. "It looks like we've got a constant bias in the—in yaw in your platform," flight controllers informed the spacemen. Instruments on the ground were recording data that indicated Snoopy had twisted about three degrees at the point where the two spacecraft were joined.

Snoopy was still go for undocking, however. But Mission Control cautioned: "If it is apparent that the LM has slipped around to about six degrees, do not undock and let's come around again and look at it."

After that transmission Apollo 10 passed behind the moon where no further communication was possible between the spacecraft and Mission Control. Until Charlie Brown and Snoopy returned to the moon's earth side, only the three astronauts would know if the undocking maneuver had been accomplished.

Forty-five minutes later the good news came from Snoopy: "We're about 30 or 40 feet away from him. Been station keeping for about 5 or 10 minutes here." The two craft had successfully undocked while they were behind the moon.

After an exchange of messages with Mission Control and the two astronauts in Snoopy, John Young fired his thrusters to move about 2,500 feet away from the smaller craft. "You will never know how big this thing gets when there ain't nobody in here but one guy," he remarked.

"You will never know how small it looks when you are as far as we are," Snoopy answered.

And Mission Control radioed: "Snoop, Charlie Brown, we see you separating on the big tube." Astronaut Young had turned on the television camera which was transmitting pictures of the buglike LM as Charlie Brown moved away.

Both Snoopy and Charlie Brown were behind the moon when Stafford and Cernan fired Snoopy's descent engine to slow the craft and lower its orbit. Snoopy's flight path would now take it to within 9.4 miles of the lunar surface at its closest point. From his own 69-mile-high orbit, John Young watched Snoopy's maneuver, ready to come to the rescue if he were needed. "They are down there among the rocks, rambling about the boulders right now," he announced jokingly when the two space vehicles emerged from behind the moon and communications were restored.

From Snoopy came an enthusiastic message: "We just saw an earth rise and it's got to be magnificent." Snoopy continued: "We'll be picking up our landing-radar test and taking pictures here—and it is a fantastic sight. They

Snoopy's view of the earth rising above the lunar horizon.

do have different shades of browns and grays here."

Snoopy had been traveling with its engine facing forward. Now the astronauts turned the vehicle to point the engine downward. With their craft in that position they were able to check the LM's landing radar which had been adjusted to lock onto the moon at 50,000 feet. That was as low as Charlie Brown could descend to rescue Stafford and Cernan in case of trouble. During a landing mission, however, the radar would begin to operate at 30,000 feet.

Stafford and Cernan were pleased with the radar. "Houston, this is Snoopy," they radioed. "It looks like this radar is doing real good."

In addition to testing the radar, the astronauts were going to inspect care-fully the area—approximately 3 miles wide and 10 miles long—that had been selected as the landing site for Apollo 11. It was the one that had looked "a little bit rugged" when they passed over it in Charlie Brown. On closer examination, they reported: "The surface actually looks very smooth, like a very wet clay, but smooth with the exception of the bigger craters."

After their 9.4-mile-high scouting pass over the Sea of Tranquillity landing site, Stafford and Cernan fired Snoopy's descent engine to increase the craft's velocity and raise the high point of its orbit. They were maneuvering toward a position in relation to the command module that would be the same as the one Apollo 11's LM would have when it left the lunar surface.

The seven-mile-wide crater Schmidt in the Sea of Tranquillity, photographed by Apollo 10 astronauts.

The two spacecraft circled the moon again with the command module in the lead. Following a second pass over the Sea of Tranquillity, the LM was scheduled to jettison its descent engine. Mission Control radioed permission to proceed with the maneuver: "Snoop, Houston. We have you go for staging."

Because John Young in Charlie Brown was more than 300 miles away from Snoopy and out of contact with the smaller craft, Mission Control kept him informed of Snoopy's progress. "Charlie Brown," Houston radioed, "they're staging. Had a wild gyration, but they got it under control."

The wild gyration was an abrupt movement that pitched Snoopy upward 50 degrees and at the same time rolled it sharply to the left just as the LM's descent stage separated from the ascent stage. A quick-reacting Astronaut Stafford wrestled with the craft's hand controls for only a few seconds before he had the pitching and rolling under control. When the crisis was over a somewhat shaken astronaut reported to Houston: "The thing just took off on us."

Investigation indicated that Snoopy's wild ride was caused by a switch which was in the wrong position. If it had been set correctly, the craft would have remained stable during the jettisoning of its descent stage. Instead, the switch turned spacecraft control over to a computer which, in turn, commanded thrusters to fire which pointed Snoopy toward Charlie Brown. In spite of this, the descent stage was successfully jettisoned, and the astronauts were ready to fire the ascent engine that would take them back to the larger spacecraft.

The first burn of the LM's ascent engine and a subsequent nudge from its thrusters placed the spacecraft in a circular orbit approximately 17 miles below the command module. From there, using the maneuvers planned for Apollo 11 when it left the moon, Astronauts Stafford and Cernan gradually overtook Charlie Brown. Soon they were able to radio Mission Control. "We're at 60 nautical miles, closing, and hard dock outlook looks real fine. I'm sure you're reading it down there. And I still don't have his flashing light from this distance of 60 miles."

A few minutes later Snoopy was calling Charlie Brown: "Okay, Charlie Brown, this is Snoopy. I'm finally starting to see your flashing light, very faintly at 42 miles, very faintly."

When Snoopy and Charlie Brown emerged from behind the moon for the last time as separated spacecraft, they were station keeping within a few feet of each other. "Okay, you ready to dock?" asked Snoopy.

John Young in Charlie Brown indicated that he was ready and Snoopy called: "Okay, John, you're in to about five feet. Looking beautiful."

"Everything looks good here," John Young answered.

Using his small maneuvering jets, Astronaut Young moved closer until the craft were joined. Twelve capture latches snapped into place and Snoopy radioed: "Hello, Houston, Snoopy and Charlie Brown are hugging each other."

During Apollo 10's seventeenth revolution of the moon Astronauts Stafford and Cernan left the LM and Charlie Brown informed Mission Control: "We're all back in the command module, the tunnel's all locked up and we're in attitude and standing by to sep here when you give us the word." The Apollo crew was ready to separate the command module from the docked lunar module which would not be needed during the remainder of the mission.

Mission Control radioed permission to undock and Charlie Brown began the countdown: "Give you a five count. Four, three, two, one. Fire! Snoopy went!" Charlie Brown announced as the two space vehicles separated.

"Are you keeping it in sight?" Mission Control asked.

"We don't have any idea where he went," Charlie Brown replied. "He just went boom and disappeared right into the sun."

Although Snoopy's departure had an unplanned velocity, probably from extra pressure in the tunnel, no harm was done and ground controllers sent the craft into orbit around the sun. "I feel sort of bad about that because he's a pretty nice guy," remarked Astronaut Cernan. "He treated us pretty well today."

Snoopy was gone but Charlie Brown remained in its 69-mile-high orbit for 14 more two-hour trips around the moon. As they traveled, the busy astronauts

Navy frogmen, balanced on the flotation collar around the Apollo 10 spacecraft, assist Astronaut Cernan onto the life raft.

took photographs of the moon's surface, practiced sighting lunar landmarks and beamed another TV program to the earth.

Charlie Brown was behind the moon on its thirty-first orbit when a two-minute burn of its SPS engine began a 54-hour homeward journey that ended in the Pacific Ocean 400 miles from Pago Pago in American Samoa. The pathfinding, 577,000-mile mission brought back hundreds of exceptionally clear photographs of the lunar surface for future Apollo crews and earthbound scientists to study. And by flying Charlie Brown to within 69 miles of the moon and testing Snoopy and its radar 50,000 feet above the moon's surface, Astronauts Tom Stafford, Gene Cernan, and John Young prepared the way for Apollo 11 and a landing on the moon.

"Today, we know we can go to the moon and we will go to the moon," said NASA Administrator Thomas O. Paine after Apollo 10 landed. "Stafford, Young, and Cernan have given us the final confidence to take the step." But Dr. Paine added a note of caution. "We will not hesitate to postpone the Apollo 11 mission if we feel we are not ready in all respects," he said. "And once the voyage has begun, we have no commitment that would make us hesitate to bring home the crew immediately if we encounter problems."

At the Kennedy Space Center a 363-foot-tall Saturn 5-Apollo spacecraft combination had already been moved into place on Launch Pad 39A for the next Apollo mission. If all went well, it was the mission that would land men on the moon.

Footprints on the Moon

U.S. Highway 1 leading to the Kennedy Space Center was unusually busy on the days preceding July 16, 1969. From all over the United States people had traveled to Florida to watch the launching of Apollo 11. For a lucky few there were seats in a grandstand area some three miles from Launch Pad 39A. But most of the spectators waited along the shoulders of the highway, on the banks of a nearby river—anywhere that they could find viewing space.

When Apollo 11 rose into the sunny Florida sky at 8:32 A.M., the hundreds of thousands of watchers saw the Saturn 5 booster's flaming tail before they heard the roar of its mighty engine because light waves travel faster than sound waves.

"There it goes!" they said. "There goes a rocket to the moon!"

The spectators saw and heard the rocket only briefly, however. Within minutes it had disappeared high over the Atlantic.

Inside the Apollo 11 space capsule were Mission Commander Neil A. Armstrong, a civilian astronaut; Air Force Colonel Edwin A. Aldrin, Jr., Apollo 11's lunar module pilot; and Air Force Lieutenant Colonel Michael Collins, the command module pilot. The three astronauts, all veterans of Project Gemini missions, kept a close watch on the spacecraft's dials and gauges. If Apollo 11 was to be a success, its many complicated systems had to be functioning perfectly prior to each of several major maneuvers leading to a landing on the moon. The go/no-go decisions would be made by flight controllers on the ground after consultation with the Apollo crew. While a no-go decision would rule out a lunar landing, it would not necessarily terminate the Apollo 11 flight. Instead, the astronauts would probably proceed with one of six alternate missions.

Apollo 11 reached its first go/no-go point after ten minutes of flight when the spacecraft was ready to begin orbiting the earth. The decision was go.

Boosted by the third stage of its Saturn 5, Apollo 11 went into a 118-mile-high orbit. After the third stage had shut down the astronauts reported: "Our insertion checklist is complete and we have no abnormalities."

During its second trip around the earth Apollo 11 faced another go/no-go decision: Should the spacecraft head for the moon or remain in earth orbit for a mission similar to Apollo 9's? Again the verdict was go.

High over the mid-Pacific the astronauts restarted the third-stage engine. It burned for 5 minutes and 20 seconds to ram the spacecraft toward the moon at 24,250 miles an hour. When the engine shut down, Commander Armstrong radioed: "Hey, Houston, Apollo 11. This Saturn gave us a magnificent ride." He added: "We have no complaints with any of the three stages on that ride. It was beautiful."

Apollo 11's speed soon slowed from its initial 24,250 miles an hour because of the backward pull of the earth's gravity. Its altitude was increasing rapidly, however, and in quick succession Mission Control had to decide if the as-

tronauts should proceed with three very important maneuvers. They were the separation of the spacecraft from the Saturn third stage, docking with the lunar module in the third stage's forward end, and removal of the LM from the third stage. After checking data on the spacecraft and the Saturn, ground control radioed: "Apollo 11, this is Houston. You're go for separation."

A few days before their historic trip to the moon, Astronauts Armstrong, Aldrin, and Collins (left to right) have much on their minds as they sit on board the transport van after the countdown test.

"We have a lift-off!" The spacecraft leaves the Kennedy Space Center's Launch Pad 39A at the beginning of man's first lunar-landing mission.

Neil Armstrong answered: "Houston, we're about to sep." And then he reported, "Separation complete."

Communications between Houston and the spacecraft were bad during the next few minutes. When Mission Control was able to contact the astronauts they were reporting: "We are docked." Apollo 11 had backed away from the Saturn third stage, turned around and joined up with the LM.

After making sure that his docking was secure and pressurizing the LM, Commander Armstrong released the four springs that held it to the third stage. "Houston, we have sep," he reported when the maneuver was completed. In four and a half hours of flight the astronauts had successfully accomplished five maneuvers that were vital to the success of the lunar landing mission.

Ground controllers started up the Saturn third-stage engine for the last time to send it past the moon and into a solar orbit. Meanwhile, Apollo 11 continued on its own three-day coast to the moon following a path so accurate that its first scheduled midcourse correction was canceled.

Compared with earlier Apollo crews, the men of Apollo 11 talked very little. "They're the quietest crew in manned space-flight history," remarked one ground controller. The astronauts did radio information of the spacecraft's systems, of course, and occasionally they described what they saw from the spacecraft. From 50,000 miles away Buzz Aldrin reported: "I can see the snow on the mountains in California." When asked if he could see Lower California in northwest Mexico, he replied: "Well, it's got some clouds up and down it."

Because of the problems experienced during earlier flights, Apollo 11's equipment included filters to remove bothersome hydrogen bubbles from the astronauts' drinking water. At the end of the first day of the flight Mike Collins reported: "It's working good so far." And Mission Commander Armstrong announced that the crew was "fit as a fiddle."

As Apollo 11 flew on toward the moon, millions of people all over the world followed its progress. They learned that a midcourse correction on July 17 was a "good burn." On July 18 they actually saw the astronauts enter the docked lunar module to begin preparations for the momentous landing on the moon.

Like previous Apollo flights, Apollo 11 carried a TV camera into space. The astronauts had already sent back views of the command module and the receding earth. Now they trained the camera on the tunnel leading to the LM to show Neil Armstrong removing Apollo 11's docking devices.

"Mike must have done a smooth job in that docking. There isn't a dent or a mark on that probe," observed Buzz Aldrin.

When the tunnel was clear, Aldrin moved the camera into the lunar module. As the LM's hatch opened, an automatic light went on inside the vehicle. "How about that! It's like a refrigerator," Mike Collins said.

For over an hour the astronauts televised the LM cabin for a worldwide audience. They showed viewers the craft's instrument panel and other equipment, and, on the cabin floor, two portable life-support systems and two helmet

As their spacecraft coasted toward a new world, the Apollo 11 astronauts photographed the receding earth.

visors in readiness for the landing on the moon.

Five hours after the conclusion of the telecast, Apollo 11 passed into the moon's sphere of influence. Its speed, which had slowed to 2,990 feet per second began to increase as the pull of lunar gravity grew stronger. The astronauts were unaware of the change recorded on their instrument panels, however, because they were asleep.

When the time approached for Apollo 11 to pass behind the moon, the astronauts were wide awake and carefully monitoring the spacecraft's dials and gauges. It was a crucial go/no-go point in the lunar mission. Before communications were blocked by the moon,

flight controllers had to decide whether Apollo 11 should start up its SPS engine to go into lunar orbit or merely swing around the moon and return to earth. Fifteen minutes before loss of signal, Mission Control radioed the spacecraft: "Eleven, this is Houston. You are go for LOI [lunar orbit insertion]."

"Roger, go for LOI," replied Buzz Aldrin in Apollo 11.

Mission Control finished the transmission with a cheerful: "All your systems are looking good going around the corner and we'll see you on the other side."

Behind the moon Apollo 11's SPS engine burned for the planned 6 minutes and 2 seconds. The thrust, against the

The docked Eagle as seen from Columbia's rendezvous window. The LM's docking window (right) is directly above the commander's position, and the markings on the window help him during docking maneuvers.

line of flight, slowed the craft and allowed it to be captured by the moon's gravity. Apollo 11 had successfully carried out another critical maneuver. Now the spacecraft was in lunar orbit and, if all went well, a lunar landing was approximately 24 hours away.

First, however, the combined spacecraft would complete 12 orbits of the moon. While the astronauts studied the lunar surface, they turned on their TV camera to send pictures to earth that included the track the LM would be following when it came in for a lunar landing. They also fired the command module's SPS engine to improve Apollo 11's orbit.

Before beginning their first rest period in lunar orbit, the astronauts gave the LM a preflight inspection. During the inspection they used the LM's code name for the first time. It was Eagle. An eagle, a symbolic emblem of the United States, was also used on the Apollo 11 insignia in the form of an eagle landing on the moon. The Apollo

"Oh, my, you guys wake up early," the astronauts replied. But they were as eager as Mission Control to begin the day's activities.

Mission Commander Armstrong and Lunar Module Pilot Aldrin were soon on their way through the tunnel to Eagle to prepare the craft for undocking. Eagle's undocking was another go/no-go point for Apollo 11. Before a decision could be reached, both spacecraft had to be examined by the astronauts who

This view of the rising earth greeted the Apollo 11 crew as their spacecraft came from behind the moon.

11 command module's name was Columbia, another national symbol. "The names are representative of the flight and the nation's hopes," Neil Armstrong explained at a pre-mission press conference.

"Apollo 11, Apollo 11, good morning!" In Houston it was 6 o'clock on the morning of July 20 and Mission Control was awakening the astronauts. If all continued to go well with the flight, it was the day for the historic landing on the moon.

also sent data to the ground for study by flight controllers. Near the end of the twelfth orbit the good news came from Mission Control: "Apollo 11, Houston. We're go for undocking."

Like Apollo 10, Apollo 11 undocked behind the moon where the astronauts were out of contact with Mission Control. When communications were restored, Neil Armstrong announced: "The Eagle has wings."

After remaining close for a few minutes to examine Eagle, Astronaut Mike

Collins, all alone now in Columbia, fired his thrusters to gradually move about two miles away. "See you later," he radioed the two astronauts in Eagle as Columbia moved off.

Before the undocked Eagle could proceed toward the lunar surface, Mission Control had to make another go/no-go decision. It involved a crucial burning of the craft's descent engine to drop Eagle into a low lunar orbit. All systems on both spacecraft were looking flight controllers on the ground. "You're go for powered descent," the latter radioed to Eagle.

Apollo 11 had successfully passed still another important go/no-go point. With a large share of the world's population tensely following their progress, Astronauts Armstrong and Aldrin restarted Eagle's engine for the trail-blazing descent to the lunar surface. Mission Control kept the world informed as Eagle's radar bounced signals off the

Mike Collins is left alone in the orbiting Columbia, while Neil Armstrong and Buzz Aldrin land on the moon. He has direct radio contact with his fellow astronauts for only a few minutes during each orbit of the command module.

good, however, and Eagle received the critical go for DOI (descent orbit insertion). The maneuver placed Eagle in an orbit that would take it to within 50,000 feet of the moon's rugged surface.

Mike Collins, who had been keeping a watchful eye on Eagle from Columbia, radioed the first word on the new orbit. "Everything's going just swimmingly," he said. Neil Armstrong and Buzz Aldrin in Eagle were pleased, too, as were moon to the craft's computer. "27,000 feet; 21,000 feet and velocity down to 12,000 feet per second; 13,500 and a velocity of 9,000 feet per second; 9,200 feet and dropping at a rate of 129 feet per second," the commentator reported.

When Eagle was less than 200 feet above the moon's surface, the astronauts realized that the craft's automatic landing system was going to bring them down in a crater littered with rocks and boulders. Moreover, a light on Eagle's instrument panel had come on to warn that only 114 seconds of fuel remained. Mission Commander Armstrong had only seconds to decide if he should abort the landing, jettison Eagle's descent stage and use its ascent engine to return to Columbia—or try to maneuver to a safe landing area. He chose to try for a landing.

Quickly taking over control from the automatic system, Armstrong guided Eagle over the Sea of Tranquillity's boulder-strewn landscape looking for a place where he could set the craft down. In addition to avoiding boulders, he had to find a fairly level surface. If Eagle landed at an angle of more than 30 degrees, it would tip over.

With less than a minute's fuel remaining, former test pilot Armstrong found what he was looking for. As he set Eagle down a cloud of dust arose, stirred by the blast of the descent engine. It was a smooth touchdown.

"Houston, Tranquillity Base here," Armstrong radioed. "The Eagle has landed." Eagle had come to rest on the lunar equator, about four miles beyond its targeted landing site.

"We're breathing again," replied Mis-

Mission Control at NASA's Manned Spacecraft Center celebrates Eagle's successful lunar landing.

sion Control as the men at the four rows of computer consoles cheered and clapped. Apollo Program Director Samuel C. Phillips spoke for all of them when he said: "In the landing phase of this mission, I was on the edge of my chair."

Mission Control relayed the good news to Mike Collins in Columbia: "He has landed—Tranquillity Base. Eagle is at Tranquillity."

From his 69-mile-high orbit a laconic Astronaut Collins replied: "Yeah, I heard the whole thing." Then he added with enthusiasm: "Fantastic!"

Although they were safely on the surface of the moon, Astronauts Armstrong and Aldrin were not yet ready to go exploring. First they had to prepare Eagle for a quick takeoff if that should become necessary. They did inspect their landing site through Eagle's windows, however. "It looks like a collection of every variety of shapes, angularities, granularities, every variety of rock you could find," they reported. "There doesn't appear to be too much of a general color at all. However, it looks as though some of the rocks and boulders —of which there are quite a few in the near area—it looks as though they're going to have some interesting colors to them."

When they finished checking Eagle, the astronauts were scheduled to begin a four-hour rest period. But they were anxious to leave the spacecraft, and after two hours of work in the lunar module they radioed Houston: "A recommendation at this point is planning an EVA with your concurrence starting about eight o'clock this evening, Hous-

ton time. That is about three hours from now."

"We will support it. We're go at that time," Houston answered.

It took another hour to make sure that Eagle's ascent stage would be able to leave the moon. Then Neil Armstrong and Edwin Aldrin began to prepare for the historic moment when they would actually set foot on the lunar surface.

The astronauts were already wearing pressure suits with a special outer layer to protect them from high temperatures and meteoroids. Now, trying to keep out of each other's way in Eagle's small cabin, they put on lunar overshoes, gloves, helmets, and backpacks. Like their suits, the overshoes, gloves, and the two visors of the helmet were designed to protect the astronauts from the hazards of extravehicular activity on the moon. The Apollo backpack, a portable life-support system (PLSS), contained an oxygen supply, water for a cooling system, communications equipment, displays and controls, and a power supply. The 84-pound PLSS was covered by a thermal insulation jacket.

It took longer than they expected for the astronauts to complete EVA preparations, but they were ready to leave Eagle six hours after landing. That was more than five hours ahead of the original schedule.

Mission Commander Neil Armstrong was the first to emerge from Eagle. After crawling through the hatch backward to the front porch, he slowly began to descend a ladder attached to one of the legs of the landing craft. On the way down he pulled a lanyard to expose a camera that televised the rest of his descent.

Perhaps as many as a billion people throughout the world saw Neil Armstrong take the historic first step on the moon. And they heard him say: "That's one small step for man, one giant leap for mankind." It was a truly awe-inspiring moment. For the first time a man was standing on the surface of another celestial body.

Astronaut Armstrong had only a moment to reflect on the significance of the occasion for he had work to do. His reports to Mission Control began at once. "The surface is fine and powdery," he radioed. "I can pick it up loosely with my toe. It does adhere in fine layers like powdered charcoal to the sole and sides

Astronaut Armstrong, with his camera mounted on a walking stick, took this close-up photograph of a few square inches of the lunar surface.

of my boots. I only go in a small fraction of an inch, maybe an eighth of an inch. But I can see the footprints of my boots and the treads in the fine sandy particles.

"There seems to be no difficulty in moving around as we suspected," Armstrong continued. "It's even perhaps easier than the simulations at one-sixth g [gravity] that we performed in the

The astronaut became so interested in simulations on the ground."
taking pictures of what he saw around him that Mission Control had to remind him several times to gather a "contingency sample." This was material that he was to scoop from the surface with a long-handled tool that had a plastic bag at its end. The filled bag was to be stored in one of his pockets. Then, if an emergency made it necessary for the astronauts to leave suddenly, they would have at least a small sample of the moon's soil and rocks for the earth's scientists.

No emergency arose, however, and after 20 minutes an impatient Buzz Aldrin, who had remained in Eagle while Mission Commander Armstrong determined if the moon's surface was safe, radioed: "Are you ready for me to come out?"

With Armstrong keeping a close watch to make sure that he didn't tear his pressure suit or his backpack, Aldrin descended Eagle's ladder to become the second man to stand on the surface of the moon. "Beautiful, beautiful!" the astronaut exclaimed as he looked around.

While Aldrin accustomed himself to walking on the moon, Armstrong mounted the 7¼-pound TV camera on a tripod and moved it about 40 feet away from Eagle. Then, as earthbound audiences watched, he unveiled a plaque on Eagle's descent stage and read: "Here men from the planet earth first set foot upon the moon, July 1969, A.D. We came in peace for all mankind." The plaque carried the signatures of the President of the United States and the Apollo crew.

As Armstrong spoke, tiny microphones inside his helmet transmitted his words to the communications unit in his backpack which, in turn, sent them to a signal processor in Eagle. Through its own small antenna Eagle beamed a voice signal to the huge dish-shaped antenna at Goldstone, California, a quarter of a million miles away. From there it went to NASA's Goddard Space Flight Center near Washington, D.C., and then to Mission Control in Houston for rebroadcast throughout the world. It also went to Astronaut Mike Collins orbiting 69 miles above the moon in Columbia. Because of his position in relation to Eagle, Collins was in direct radio contact with the moon explorers for only a few minutes during each orbit.

Eagle's transmitter also sent out TV signals from the black-and-white camera that the astronauts had set up on the moon, but those signals were received at Parkes, Australia, rather than Goldstone.

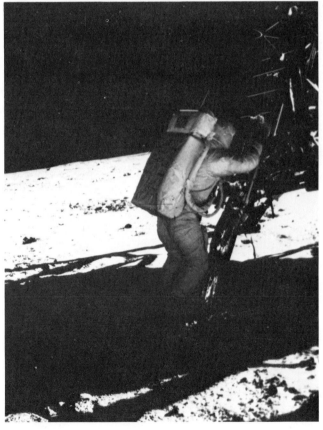

Astronaut Aldrin descends the lunar module ladder to become the second man to set foot upon the surface of the moon.

When the two astronauts talked with one another on the moon, they did so by radio, using receivers and transmitters in their backpacks.

The first men on the moon quickly became accustomed to the weak lunar gravity and they learned how to handle the weight of their backpacks. "Got to be careful that you are leaning in the direction you want to go," observed Astronaut Aldrin. Later he had this to say about walking on the moon: "I found that a standard loping technique of one foot in front of the other worked out quite well as we would have expected. One could also jump in more of a kangaroo fashion, two feet at a time. This seemed to work, but without quite the same degree of control of your stability as you moved along. We found that we had to anticipate three to four steps in comparison with the one or two steps that are ahead when you're walking on the earth."

Loping over the lunar surface without any visible effort, Aldrin returned to Eagle and removed a solar wind collector from the craft's external storage area. It was an aluminum-foil screen designed to trap particles streaming in from the sun. Scientists hoped that the screen would enable them to determine the solar wind's composition. Aldrin set it up not far from Eagle.

Although millions of TV viewers on earth were watching the two astronauts on the moon, Mike Collins in the orbiting Columbia was unable to see them. "How's it going?" he asked Mission Control.

"The EVA is going beautifully," Mission Control replied. "I believe they are setting up the flag now. . . . They've got the flag up and you can see the Stars and Stripes on the lunar surface."

Astronaut Armstrong had planted a 3-by-5-foot American flag not far from Eagle. Wire held the flag outstretched in the airless atmosphere of the moon. Planting the flag was merely a symbolic gesture, however. The United States was not laying claim to the moon. The 1967 Space Treaty, to which the United States is a party, opened the moon to exploration by all countries.

After the flag was in place, the astronauts received a message from Mission Control: "The President of the United States is in his office now and would like to say a few words to you."

"That would be an honor," Neil Armstrong replied.

The astronauts were standing in front of their TV camera when the President said: "Neil and Buzz, I am talking to you by telephone from the Oval Room at the White House. And this certainly has to be the most historic telephone call ever made. I just can't tell you how proud we all are of what you—for every American, this has to be the proudest day of our lives. And for people all over the world, I am sure they, too, join with Americans in recognizing what a feat this is. Because of what you have done, the heavens have become a part of man's world. And as you talk to us from the Sea of Tranquillity, it inspires us to double our efforts to bring peace and tranquillity to earth. For one priceless moment, in the whole history of man, all the people on this earth are truly one. One in their pride in what you have done. And one in our prayers that you will return safely to earth."

Neil Armstrong answered for the as-

President Nixon in the White House talks to Astronauts Armstrong and Aldrin on the moon. Right: *The astronauts responding, as seen on television at the time.*

tronauts. "Thank you, Mr. President," he said. "It's a great honor and privilege for us to be here representing not only the United States but men of peace of all nations. And with interest and a curiosity and a vision for the future. It's an honor for us to be able to participate here today."

Following their talk with the President the busy astronauts resumed their lunar tasks. While Aldrin took pictures and examined Eagle, Armstrong gathered rocks and soil which he placed in a sample-return container. Apollo 11's two "rock boxes" were 19 inches long, 11½ inches wide, and 8 inches high.

Each one was hollowed out of a single aluminum block. Armstrong used a long-handled scoop to gather the soil and rocks because it would have been impossible for him to bend down far enough in his pressure suit.

Next, the astronauts removed the Early Apollo Scientific Experiments Package (EASEP) from Eagle's external equipment bay. The EASEP consisted of a very sensitive seismometer and a set of mirrors to reflect back to earth the laser beams that scientists planned to send to the moon. By measuring the length of time it took the laser beams to return to earth, they hoped to measure accu-

Above: *Buzz Aldrin removes the EASEP from the scientific equipment bay in Eagle's descent stage.* Right: *He stands near the solar wind collector which he has just erected.*

rately the distance between the two bodies.

The seismometer, by registering moonquakes, would help scientists determine if the moon had a solid interior, or a molten one like the earth. The astronauts set up the experiments about 30 feet from Eagle.

When Neil Armstrong had been on the moon's surface for an hour and 50 minutes and Buzz Aldrin 20 minutes less than that, Mission Control radioed: "Buzz, this is Houston. You've got about ten minutes left now prior to commencing your EVA termination activities." Aldrin was to re-enter Eagle

first. Before he went back inside, however, he helped Armstrong gather more lunar samples for the earth's scientists. The astronauts were supposed to note where they found the rocks in the final collection, but there wasn't time to keep a record.

"Neil, Buzz," Mission Control radioed. "Let's press on with getting the close-up camera magazine and closing out the sample-return container. We're running a little low on time." The astronauts' backpacks had enough oxygen for four hours on the moon, but the flight controllers wanted to maintain an adequate safety margin.

After placing the solar wind experiment and some soil samples in a rock box, Aldrin headed up Eagle's ladder with a cheerful: "Adios, amigo." From the spacecraft's hatch he helped Armstrong manipulate a pulley system to raise the two sealed rock boxes which he lifted into the cabin. Twenty minutes later Armstrong joined Aldrin in Eagle. "The hatch is closed and latched," they reported to Mission Control.

The first men to walk on the moon had returned to their spacecraft. They left evidence of their visit behind them, however. The American flag still stood where they had placed it. The seismometer and laser experiments remained, as did 73 microfilmed messages from the world's leaders, and medals and shoulder patches belonging to Virgil Grissom, Roger Chaffee, Edward White, Yuri Gagarin, and Vladimir Komarov, American and Soviet spacemen who had died. There was some lunar litter as well. The astronauts discarded their TV camera, boots, backpacks, and other items they no longer needed. And their footprints remained on the lunar surface to record where they had walked during man's greatest adventure.

After lift-off from the lunar surface, Eagle approaches the orbiting Columbia.

Two tired, but happy, astronauts settled down in Eagle's small cabin after the historic first visit to the lunar surface. That part of the Apollo 11 mission had been an unqualified success. But the mission was far from over. Ahead lay several difficult and possibly dangerous maneuvers: a blast-off from the moon, a redocking with the orbiting Columbia, a long journey back to earth, and a landing in the Pacific Ocean. Before they attempted to leave the moon, however, the astronauts carefully rechecked Eagle's systems. They also ate and tried to rest. The rest period lasted seven

hours, but they found it difficult to sleep in Eagle's cramped, couchless cabin. Armstrong curled up on the craft's engine cover. Aldrin chose the floor.

Columbia was in its twenty-fifth revolution of the moon when Mission Control radioed to Eagle: "You're cleared for takeoff."

Eagle answered: "Roger, understand. We're number 1 on the runway."

Some 21 hours after landing on the moon and 12½ hours after the memorable moon walk, Flight Commander Armstrong was ready to start up Eagle's ascent engine. It was one of the most suspense-filled moments of the entire mission. If the engine failed to ignite, the astronauts would have to remain on the moon. There was no way to rescue them before their oxygen supply ran out because Columbia could come no lower than 50,000 feet. And if Eagle's engine did start, but shut down too soon, the craft would come crashing back to the lunar surface.

"Forward 8, 7, 6, 5, abort stage, engine arm ascent, proceed. That was beautiful!" called Armstrong as Eagle's ascent stage rose from the lunar surface. Its descent stage, which had served as a launching pad, remained on the moon.

"Eagle, Houston," radioed a relieved Mission Control, "one minute and you're looking good."

After a seven-minute climb, Eagle's engine shut down and the craft went into a low lunar orbit. From there Eagle would gradually maneuver back to Columbia, now orbiting 50 miles above and 300 miles ahead of the lunar module.

When the two spacecraft swung around to the earth side of the moon on Columbia's twenty-seventh revolution, only a few feet separated them and minutes later they were docked. "Everything is going fine," announced Mike Collins in Columbia.

Before crawling through the tunnel to rejoin Astronaut Collins in Columbia, Neil Armstrong and Buzz Aldrin carefully removed any moon dust that might be clinging to their clothing and the equipment they were bringing with them. This was part of an elaborate procedure NASA had devised to prevent contamination by unknown lunar organisms against which life on earth might have no defense. The astronauts had already discarded their boots (the item most likely to be contaminated), TV camera, and backpacks. They left some of their remaining equipment—things for which they had no further need—in Eagle and transferred the rest, including their spacesuits, helmets, watches, and the two rock boxes, to Columbia in sealed bags.

Once the two lunar explorers were back in Columbia, they radioed Mission Control: "We're all three back inside. The hatch is installed. We're running a pressure-leak check. Everything going well."

Eagle, the first manned spacecraft to land on the moon, had finished its part of the Apollo 11 mission. The astronauts jettisoned the sturdy craft into a lunar orbit and began preparations for their own return to earth.

With Eagle gone, Columbia became Apollo 11 again. "Apollo 11," Mission Control radioed after checking data from the spacecraft, "you are go for TEI [trans-earth injection]." Like Apollo 8 and Apollo 10 before it, Apollo 11 had received permission to perform the tricky maneuver that would send it hurtling toward the earth along a precise path leading to a safe landing in the Pacific.

When Apollo 11 was behind the moon at the beginning of the thirty-first revolution, the astronauts started up their powerful SPS engine and kept it going for 2½ minutes. At the end of the burn, which used up 10,000 pounds of propellant, the spacecraft was traveling away from the moon at a speed of 8,660 feet per second.

"All your systems look real good to

us," Mission Control radioed when Apollo 11 emerged from behind the moon.

"That was a beautiful burn," replied Astronaut Armstrong. "They don't come any finer."

Now that Apollo 11 was safely on its way back to earth, sleep became the first order of business for the astronauts. Neil Armstrong and Buzz Aldrin were especially tired because they had not slept well during their "night" in Eagle.

The astronauts were back at work again after a 10-hour rest when Apollo 11 left the moon's sphere of influence. Its speed, which had dropped to 3,994 feet per second, began to increase as the pull of the earth's gravity grew stronger.

had something new to show their worldwide audience. Directing the camera at two oblong objects lashed to the cabin floor, Neil Armstrong said: "These two boxes are the sample-return containers. They're vacuum-packed containers that were closed in a vacuum on the lunar surface, sealed, and then brought inside the LM and then put inside these fiberglass bags, zippered, and resealed around the outside and placed in these receptacles in the side of the command module."

Mike Collins had something to show the younger members of the TV audience. "This next is a little demonstration for the kids at home, all kids everywhere for that matter," he said. "I was going to show you how you drink water out of a spoon, but I'm afraid I filled the spoon too full and if I'm not careful, I'm going to spill water right over the sides. Can you see the water slopping around on the top of the spoon, kids?

"Okay. Well, as I said, I was going to tell you, but I'm afraid I filled it too far and it's going to spill over the sides. I'll tell you what. I'll just turn this one over and get rid of the water and start all over again. Okay?

"And you can see up here we don't know where over is," Collins observed as the water remained in the upturned spoon. He pushed the water off with his finger and blew at it as it hung in the gravity-free cabin. The astronaut finally disposed of the water by catching it in his mouth.

The next day, which was their last full day in space, the astronauts sent another TV program to earth. The historic voyage to the moon was nearing

Back inside Eagle after his moon walk, Astronaut Aldrin is tired but very happy.

Although more than 180,000 miles still separated them from the earth, one of the space travelers remarked: "Nice to sit here and watch the earth grow larger and larger and the moon smaller and smaller."

When the Apollo 11 crew turned on the command module's TV camera for the first time on the return journey, they its end and they wanted to share some of their thoughts with the millions of people who had followed their adventures. Astronaut Neil Armstrong introduced the program.

"A hundred years ago Jules Verne wrote a book about a voyage to the moon," he said. "His spaceship, Columbia, took off from Florida and landed in the Pacific Ocean after completing a trip to the moon. It seems appropriate to us to share with you some of the reflections of the crew as the modern-day Columbia completes its rendezvous with the planet earth and the same Pacific Ocean tomorrow."

Astronaut Michael Collins was the next to appear on the TV screen. "This trip of ours to the moon may have looked, to you, simple or easy," he said. "I'd like to say that it has not been a game.

"The Saturn 5 rocket which put us into orbit is an incredibly complicated piece of machinery, every piece of which worked flawlessly. This computer up above my head has a 38,000-word vocabulary, each word of which has been very carefully chosen to be of the utmost value to us, the crew. This switch which I have in my hand now has over 300 counterparts in the command module alone. . . . In addition to that, there are myriads of circuit breakers, levers, rods, and other associated controls. The SPS engine, our large rocket engine on the aft end of our service module, must have performed flawlessly or we would have been stranded in lunar orbit. The parachutes up above my head must work perfectly tomorrow, or we will plummet into the ocean.

"We have always had confidence that all this equipment will work, and work

On their way back to earth, the Apollo 11 astronauts photographed the full moon which they had just visited.

properly, and we continue to have confidence that it will do so for the remainder of the flight. All this is possible only through the blood, sweat, and tears of a number of people. First, the American workmen who put these pieces of machinery together in the factory. Second, the painstaking work done by the various test teams during the assembly and retest after assembly. And finally, the people at the Manned Spacecraft Center, both in management, in mission planning, in flight control, and last, but not least, in crew training.

"This operation is somewhat like the periscope of a submarine," Astronaut Collins concluded. "All you see is the three of us, but beneath the surface are thousands and thousands of others, and to all those I would like to say thank you very much."

When Astronaut Edwin Aldrin came on, he said: "I'd like to discuss with you a few of the more symbolic aspects of the flight, of our mission, Apollo 11. We've been discussing the events that have taken place in the past two or three days here on board our spacecraft. We've come to the conclusion that this has been far more than three men on a voyage to the moon. More still than the efforts of a government and industry team. More even than the efforts of one nation. We feel that this stands as a symbol of the insatiable curiosity of all mankind to explore the unknown. Neil's statement the other day upon first setting foot on the surface of the moon, 'This is a small step for a man, but a great leap for mankind,' I believe sums up these feelings very nicely."

Mission Commander Armstrong con-

This woman making ear cups for the astronauts' headsets is one of thousands of workers who contributed to the Apollo program.

cluded the program by saying: "We would like to give a special thanks to all those Americans who built the spacecraft, who did the construction, design, the tests, and put their hearts and all their abilities into those crafts. To those people tonight we give a special thank you, and to all the other people that are listening and watching tonight, God bless you. Good night from Apollo 11."

When Apollo 11 was 19,000 miles from the earth and traveling toward it at a speed of 14,633 feet per second, Mission Control radioed: "The *Hornet* is on station just far enough off the target point to keep from getting hit. Recovery 1, the chopper, is there. They are on station and Hawaii Rescue 1 and 2, the C130s [rescue aircraft], are within 40 minutes of your target point." The recovery force was ready and waiting for the spacecraft's touchdown in the Pacific Ocean near Johnston Island.

As it sped toward the earth, traveling right down the middle of its re-entry corridor, Apollo 11's speed reached an incredible 36,237 feet per second—more than 24,000 miles an hour—just before it re-entered the atmosphere. The six-ton command module was all that remained of Apollo 11 because the astronauts had jettisoned the service module as part of their preparations for landing.

Heat generated by its passage through the thickening atmosphere cut off Apollo 11's radio contact with the earth, but excited watchers on the deck of the *Hornet* heard a sonic boom as the spacecraft approached. They also caught a brief glimpse of Apollo 11's three 83-foot-diameter orange and white parachutes. Among the watchers was Presi-

dent Richard Nixon who had traveled to the *Hornet* to greet the returning astronauts.

Apollo 11 landed in the Pacific nine miles from the *Hornet* 195 hours, 18 minutes, and 21 seconds after leaving the Kennedy Space Center on its historic voyage to the moon. Frogmen quickly attached a flotation collar and two rafts to the bobbing craft. "Our condition is all three excellent," reported Mike Collins from inside the capsule.

It was some minutes before the astronauts entered the rafts. First they put on biological isolation garments, green coveralls with gasmask-like filters for the face, that one of the frogmen tossed through the hatch. When they finally did emerge from the spacecraft, there was another delay while the frogman scrubbed down their coveralls with a disinfectant. He also scrubbed down the area around the hatch. Like the precautions already taken by the astronauts, these measures were part of NASA's attempt to guard against contamination of the earth by lunar organisms.

In spite of the magnitude of their accomplishment, the danger of contamination ruled out a welcoming ceremony for the Apollo 11 crew when they arrived on the *Hornet*. Instead, they moved directly from the recovery helicopter to the Mobile Quarantine Facility (MQF) on the *Hornet's* hanger deck. The MQF was a sealed van that resembled a house trailer without wheels.

Space Administration physicians had decided that 21 days would provide enough time for symptoms to develop if the astronauts did indeed harbor moon germs. Therefore, when the astronauts left the moon they had begun a 21-day

A frogman secures the hatch of the Apollo 11 spacecraft, while the three astronauts wait in a life raft for a helicopter to pick them up. All are wearing the biological isolation garments required by the Apollo quarantine program.

quarantine period which they now continued in the MQF. They were not completely cut off from the rest of the world in the hermetically sealed van. A doctor and a technician joined them in quarantine and the astronauts were able to communicate with the outside world through microphones and loudspeakers.

The Apollo 11 crew returned to the Manned Spacecraft Center in Houston without ever leaving the MQF. The *Hornet* carried the MQF to Hawaii where it was transferred to an airplane for the rest of the journey. At the Manned Spacecraft Center, the astronauts moved into a $15 million Lunar Receiving Laboratory (LRL), a low concrete building especially constructed to house men and materials newly arrived from the moon. Apollo 11's two rock boxes had already been flown to the LRL.

While the most exciting part of Apollo 11 was undoubtedly the fact that

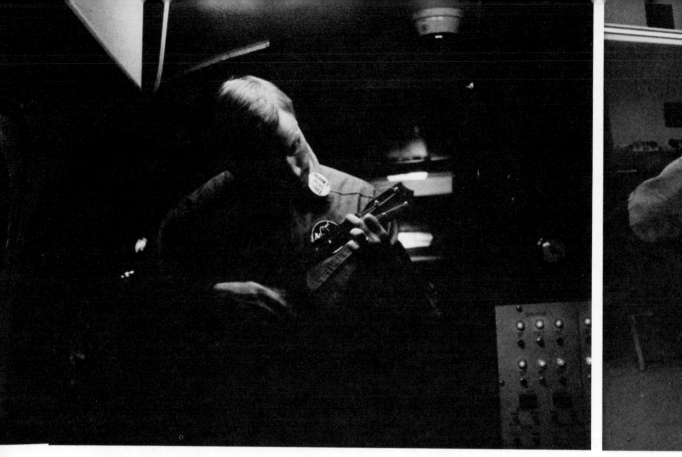

Inside the Mobile Quarantine Facility, Neil Armstrong plays a ukelele and relaxes after his momentous mission.

men had walked on the surface of the moon, the excitement was by no means over. There was much to be learned from the astronauts now that they were back on earth and perhaps even more from the 47.6 pounds of lunar samples that they collected.

The two boxes containing lunar rocks and soil were opened in a small chamber with a vacuum similar to that of the moon. In order to preserve the vacuum and to protect the rocks and soil from contamination, NASA's technicians did not enter the chamber. Instead they worked through a pair of gloves set in the wall of the chamber while eager scientists watched through a glass porthole.

Twenty-six scientists, NASA's Preliminary Examination Team, were the first to study the long-awaited lunar samples. When they finished, the rocks and soil were distributed among another group of scientists, called Principal Investigators, for a more detailed analysis.

While Apollo 11's rock boxes didn't contain the answers to every question about the moon, scientists were able to learn a great deal about the nature and composition of lunar surface materials. Meanwhile, after some initial difficulty, other scientists succeeded in bouncing the first laser beams from the reflector left on the moon by the Apollo crew. And the seismometer also left there registered a series of slight lunar tremors.

Three weeks after they landed on the moon, Neil Armstrong, Edwin Aldrin, and Michael Collins emerged from quarantine. Dr. Berry, the astronauts'

Scientists at the Lunar Receiving Laboratory wanted to keep the moon rocks in a vacuum similar to that on the moon. They examined them using gloves set in the wall of a vacuum chamber.

physician, announced that they were "perfectly healthy." No signs of lunar organisms had been detected in them or in the rocks and soil they brought back.

At their first press conference after leaving quarantine, reporters asked the astronauts for their personal reactions to the historic landing on the moon. Speaking first, Edwin Aldrin said: "Well, I believe that what this country set out to do was something that was going to be done sooner or later whether we set a specific goal or not. I believe that from the early space flights we demonstrated a potential to carry out this type of mission. And again it was a question of time until this would be accomplished. I think the relative ease with which we were able to carry out our mission—which, of course, came after a very efficient and logical sequence of flights—I think that this demonstrated that we were certainly on the right track when we took this commitment to go to the moon. I think that what this means is that many other problems perhaps can be solved in the same way—by taking a commitment to solve them in a long-time fashion."

"To me there are near- and far-term aspects to it," Michael Collins said of the landing on the moon. "On the near term, I think it a technical triumph for this country to have said what it was going to do a number of years ago and then, by golly, do it—just like we said we were going to do. Not just, perhaps, purely technical, but also a triumph for the nation's overall determination, will, economy, attention to detail, and a thousand and one other factors that went into it. That's short term. I think, long term, we find for the first time that man has the flexibility, or the option, of either

133

walking this planet or some other planet, be it the moon or Mars, or I don't know where. And I'm poorly equipped to evaluate where that may lead us to."

And Apollo 11 Commander Neil Armstrong, the man who took the first step on the moon, said: "I see it as a beginning. Not just this flight, but in this program which has really been a very short piece of human history. An instant in history, the entire program. It's a beginning of a new age."

Potential moon explorers study a two-pound moon rock at the Smithsonian Institution.

A New Age of Space Exploration

With the trail-blazing Apollo 11 flight, the United States achieved its space goal. Americans had landed on the moon and returned safely to earth during the decade of the 1960s. Project Apollo was not over, however. NASA planned to send eight more Apollo missions to the moon.

Apollo 12 left the Kennedy Space Center's Pad 39A on November 14, 1969, during a heavy rainstorm. It was a launching that gave the Apollo 12 crew—Mission Commander Charles (Pete) Conrad, Jr., Command Module Pilot Richard F. Gordon, and Lunar Module Pilot Alan L. Bean—some uneasy moments. The spacecraft experienced a sudden power failure shortly after lift-off.

Apparently, Apollo 12 had been struck by lightning from the clouds that hung over the launch site. Lightning was seen by observers on the ground, although the astronauts noticed only a glow outside their windows. The spacecraft's power was restored within a few seconds and, after making sure no damage had been done, the astronauts continued on their way to the moon.

During the first part of its lunar journey Apollo 12 used procedures already tested by Apollo 8, Apollo 10, and Apollo 11. Some 31 hours after lift-off, however, Apollo 12 Commander Pete Conrad altered the spacecraft's course. Instead of continuing along a path that would allow a "free return" to earth in case his SPS engine failed to start behind the moon, Conrad set off on a "hybrid" trajectory. It, too, would permit a single swing around the moon in case of engine failure. But on the return journey Apollo 12 might miss the earth by as much as 56,000 miles.

The new course was designed to bring Apollo 12's lunar module, Intrepid, to the moon's Ocean of Storms when the spacecraft was in contact with the tracking antenna at Goldstone, California, and when lighting conditions were ideal for a pinpoint landing.

An accurate landing was important for two reasons. If Apollo 12 hit its target, future Apollo missions could move on to regions of the moon where rough terrain made precise touchdowns a necessity. And NASA wanted Apollo 12 to come down close enough to the crater where the unmanned Surveyor 3 had landed in 1967 for the astronauts to examine that craft. The crater was approximately 950 miles west of Apollo 11's Tranquillity Base.

Intrepid's landing in the moon's Ocean of Storms at 1:54 A.M. on November 19 was a masterpiece of accuracy. Former Navy pilot Pete Conrad, assisted by Alan Bean, brought the lunar module down only 20 feet from the edge of Surveyor 3's crater. That craft was one of the first things Conrad saw after he emerged from Intrepid to become the third man to set foot on the moon.

"Guess what I see sitting on the side of the crater? The old Surveyor!" the delighted astronaut radioed to Alan Bean, who had not yet left the lunar module.

While Astronaut Richard Gordon in the command module, Yankee Clipper, circled the moon in a 69-mile-high orbit,

Astronauts Conrad and Bean began a busy period of EVA on the moon's surface. They erected an American flag, set up a screen to trap solar-wind particles, and deployed an Apollo Lunar Surface Experiments Package (ALSEP).

Apollo 12's ALSEP was more complex than Apollo 11's EASEP. It consisted of a seismometer to detect lunar quakes; a solar-wind spectrometer to measure the energy, velocity, and direction of the solar wind; a magnetometer to measure the moon's magnetic fields; a lunar-atmosphere detector to measure the moon's meager atmosphere; and a lunar-ionosphere detector to identify electrically charged atoms near the moon's surface. After setting up the devices, the astronauts connected them to a nuclear-powered battery designed to keep them running for at least a year.

As they moved about on the lunar surface, Conrad and Bean paused frequently to collect rocks for the earth's scientists. The astronauts carefully photographed the rocks and described them and other features of the lunar terrain. Their descriptions were especially important because Intrepid's color-TV camera had stopped working early in the moon walk. Possibly a sensitive vidicon tube had burned out when the camera was inadvertently pointed at the sun. The astronauts tried to repair the camera, but their efforts were unsuccessful.

After four hours on the lunar surface, Pete Conrad and Alan Bean returned to Intrepid. They were not through exploring the moon, however. Twelve hours later the white-suited astronauts re-emerged from Intrepid. This time they moved farther away from the

One of the Apollo 12 astronauts approaches Surveyor 3. Intrepid is about 600 feet away on the rim of the crater.

spacecraft, collecting rock samples, taking photographs, and recording descriptions of the terrain as they went.

Following a meandering path that allowed them to examine four small craters, the astronauts finally came to the 650-foot-wide crater in which Surveyor 3 had landed. They reported of the once blue-and-white Surveyor: "It's all tan. The sun has cooked it. It's changed to brown."

After examining the Surveyor, Conrad and Bean removed the craft's TV camera, some glass, tubing and cables, and the scoop that Surveyor had used to test lunar soil. The parts had been on the moon for two and a half years and scientists were eager to learn how the harsh lunar conditions had affected them.

Carrying the Surveyor components and the rock samples they had collected, the astronauts returned to their spacecraft at the conclusion of their second four hours of lunar exploration. Intrepid lifted off from the moon at 9:26 A.M. on November 20 after 31½ hours on the lunar surface. Three hours later, Intrepid was successfully docked with Yankee Clipper.

After Astronauts Conrad and Bean had crawled back into Yankee Clipper, the two craft were undocked. Then from Yankee Clipper the astronauts sent a radio signal that restarted Intrepid's engine to send that craft crashing back to the surface of the moon. It landed some 40 miles from the seismometer in the Ocean of Storms, causing the instrument to register a tremor that lasted 55 minutes. Amazed scientists pointed out that a similar impact on earth would have produced a tremor that lasted no more than a minute.

Apollo 12 landed in the Pacific Ocean on November 24, ending the second U.S. manned mission to the surface of the moon. The Apollo 12 astronauts demonstrated that a precise landing on the moon was possible and they took the first steps toward extending the range of man's activities on the moon's surface. Apollo 12's 90 pounds of lunar rocks and soil, its photographs and recorded observations, and its experiments added important information to that already gained from the pioneer Apollo 11. Both helped prepare the way for later Apollo missions when astronauts would land on rough lunar terrain and spend more time on the moon. They would set up more complex experiments and bring back a greater variety of rock and soil samples. Apollo astronauts may eventually travel as far as three miles from their lunar modules using a four-wheeled "rover," an electrically-driven vehicle especially designed for excursions on the moon.

American astronauts may someday share the exploration of the moon with Soviet cosmonauts. The Soviet Union has sent several unmanned spacecraft to the moon on missions similar to those of NASA's Rangers, Surveyors, and Lunar Orbiters. One of the Soviet Union's unmanned craft, Luna 15, was traveling to the moon at the same time as Apollo 11. It completed 52 orbits and landed two hours before the Apollo 11 astronauts took off in Eagle for the return journey to Columbia. The Apollo 11 crew was kept informed of Luna 15's movements, but the astronauts did not see the

An Apollo 12 astronaut uses a core sampler to collect lunar soil. Next to him is a tool rack.

Russian craft. It was too far away.

The Soviet Union has conducted a very successful space effort involving manned as well as unmanned missions. It was the Soviet Union's Sputnik 1 that inaugurated the space age on October 4, 1957, and Soviet Cosmonaut Yuri Gagarin who made the first manned space flight on April 12, 1961. On August 6, 1961, the Soviet Union followed up Gagarin's single-orbit mission with one that remained aloft for 17 orbits of the earth. Its pilot, Cosmonaut Gherman Titov, slept and ate three meals during his journey. His spacecraft was a Vostok (*East*) similar to the one flown by Gagarin.

In August, 1962, two Soviet cosmonauts became the first to fly formation in space when Andrian Nikolayev and Pavel Popovich flew to within four miles of one another while orbiting the earth in two Vostoks. In June, 1963, another Soviet cosmonaut, Valery Bykovsky, spent five days in earth orbit in Vostok 5. Launched just two days after Bykovsky, Valentina Tereshkova, the world's first woman space traveler, remained in orbit for three days in Vostok 6.

At the time of the Vostok 5 and 6 flights, the longest United States space flight was Astronaut Gordon Cooper's 34-hour Mercury 9 mission. Unlike the Soviet Union, the United States had not yet developed rockets. capable of boosting heavy loads into space. As a result, its spacecraft were smaller than the 10,000-pound Vostoks and they could not carry enough oxygen and other supplies for long stays in space.

Because of its larger boosters, the Soviet Union was able to send a three-man spacecraft aloft before the United States launched its first two-man Gemini mission. The Soviet Voskhod 1 (*Sunrise*), launched on October 12, 1964, on a 16-orbit flight, carried Vladimir Komarov, who piloted the craft, Boris Yegorov, a space doctor, and Konstantin Feoktistov, a scientist. Voskhod 2, launched on March 18, 1965, had two passengers, Cosmonauts Pavel Belyayev and Aleksei Leonov. During the 17-orbit flight Leonov left the crew cabin to become the first man to "walk" in space.

On April 23, 1967, the Soviet Union launched a 15,000-pound spacecraft called Soyuz 1 (*Union*). It crashed after a troubled flight, killing its pilot, Cosmonaut Vladimir Komarov. After Soyuz 1, there were no more Soviet manned space flights until October, 1968, when Soyuz 3 remained in earth orbit for four days. During that time Cosmonaut Georgi Beregovoi rendezvoused twice with Soyuz 2, an unmanned capsule. He did not try to dock with it, however.

With Soyuz 4 and Soyuz 5, launched on January 14 and 15, 1969, the Soviets demonstrated that they had mastered a docking technique that could be used by cosmonauts traveling to space stations or to the moon. Soyuz 4 carried Cosmonaut Vladimir Shatalov; in Soyuz 5 were Cosmonauts Boris Volynov, Aleksei Yeliseyev, and Yevgini Khrunov. While the two capsules were docked, Yeliseyev and Khrunov left Soyuz 5, walked over to Soyuz 4 and entered that craft for the journey back to earth. It was the first passenger exchange in space.

Beginning on October 11, 1969, the Soviet Union launched Soyuz 6, Soyuz 7, and Soyuz 8 into earth orbit on successive days. Two of the craft rendez-

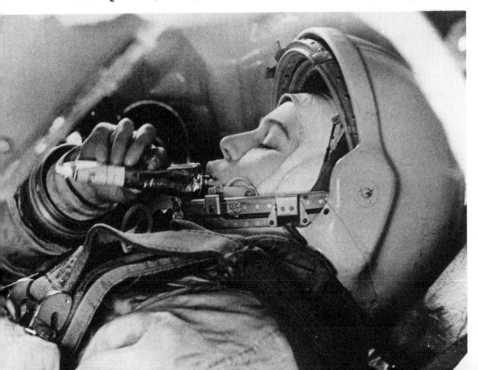

Cosmonaut Valentina Tereshkova, the world's first space woman, eats food from a tube.

voused, but they did not dock. Seven cosmonauts took part in the week-long mission.

The Soviet Union does not publicize its plans for exploring space. However, the Soyuz flights and several successful unmanned lunar missions indicate that cosmonauts will be landing on the moon. In addition, Soviet plans for the future probably include manned stations in earth and in lunar orbit and manned missions to Mars and possibly Venus. Unmanned Soviet craft will continue to go to the moon, Mars, and Venus and they will go to more distant planets as well. Soviet scientists may also be planning an unmanned lunar laboratory.

United States plans for the new age of space exploration begin with the Apollo Applications Program. It will use a Saturn 5 rocket to boost a space station into a near-earth orbit. The space station, actually the empty third stage of a Saturn 5, will provide a laboratory measuring 21 feet in diameter and 58 feet in length. A three-man team of astronauts will set up the laboratory and a large solar telescope during a mission lasting 28 days. Three more astronauts will spend another 56 days in the laboratory observing the earth's weather, oceans, forests, agriculture, and geography and conducting other studies. A last group of three astronauts will make a 56-day visit to the laboratory to continue the observations and studies.

When the Apollo Applications Program is concluded, NASA hopes to establish a permanent space station to which as many as a hundred astronauts and scientists will travel in a new kind of space shuttle. The shuttle, launched by a rocket, would return to earth under its own power and land at an airport.

Sometime after the last Apollo flight to the moon, the United States may establish a small lunar base for scientists who wish to conduct astronomical studies on the moon where there is no atmosphere to distort what they see through their telescopes. Before carrying out that project, however, NASA plans to place a space station in orbit around the moon. From 6 to 12 astronauts will live in the station for as long as a year. They will receive supplies from the earth at regular intervals. From time to time astronauts will descend to the moon in a lunar lander and remain there from two to four weeks. In addition to exploring and setting up experiments, they will collect samples to be analyzed in the orbiting space station.

When the time comes to establish a semi-permanent base on the moon, NASA may bring in a nuclear power station. If there is water in the form of ice below the lunar surface, as some scientists think, power will be needed to separate the water into oxygen and hydrogen to supply an atmosphere for breathing and propellants for traveling to and from the orbiting lunar station.

Sometime in the 1980s, or later, the United States will land astronauts on Mars. It will be a tremendous undertaking. The astronauts will have to travel 60 million miles to reach Mars, a voyage that could take 270 or more days depending on the method used. Moreover, landing on Mars might cost as much as $100 billion compared with the $24 billion that Project Apollo spent to land astronauts on the moon.

In spite of the difficulties and expense that will be encountered in reaching it,

Mars is the logical next step after the exploration of the moon. Unmanned probes to the vicinity of Mars have indicated that its temperature, atmosphere, and surface conditions, while inhospitable, would not prevent man from operating there. Furthermore, the distance to Mars is not prohibitive as it is with some of the other planets. NASA is already working on a NERVA (Nuclear Engine for Rocket Vehicle Application) rocket system that could power a manned mission to Mars, and the post-Apollo space-station projects will provide experience in keeping men alive in space for extended periods of time.

While its astronauts and scientists are working on plans for a manned mission to Mars, NASA will send unmanned spacecraft to investigate that planet and other planets as well. Mariner satellites have already sent back valuable pictures and scientific data from the vicinity of Mars. Additional Mariners and other unmanned spacecraft, such as the Viking, will continue to examine Mars just as Ranger, Surveyor, and Lunar Orbiter spacecraft scouted the moon for Project Apollo.

Now that man has gone to the moon, it is inevitable that he will continue to explore the universe in which he lives. The scope of that exploration will depend on scientific and technical advances and the funds that can be spared from urgent needs on earth, but the important first step has been taken. When the brave men of Project Apollo landed on the surface of the moon, they began a new age of space exploration.

One of the Apollo 12 moon explorers holds a sample container. His fellow explorer—who took this photograph—is reflected in his visor.

Appendix

The Apollo Astronauts

Edwin E. Aldrin, Jr.—Astronaut Edwin E. Aldrin, Jr., Apollo 11's lunar module pilot and one of the first two men to walk on the moon, was born in Montclair, New Jersey, on January 20, 1930. He graduated from the U.S. Military Academy at West Point before joining the Air Force.

After spending several years as an Air Force pilot, Aldrin, whose nickname is "Buzz," earned a doctor of science degree in astronautics at the Massachusetts Institute of Technology. He wrote his doctoral thesis on guidance techniques for orbital rendezvous, a subject that was to play an important part in Project Gemini and Project Apollo.

When he became an astronaut in 1963, Aldrin was assigned to the Air Force Field Office at NASA's Manned Spacecraft Center. Subsequently, he served as pilot of the Gemini 12 flight, during which he made a space walk that lasted more than two hours. He has helped plan missions for both Project Gemini and Project Apollo.

William A. Anders—William A. Anders was born in Hong Kong on October 17, 1933. His father was stationed in Hong Kong with the U.S. Navy.

After graduating from the U.S. Naval Academy, the future astronaut became an Air Force pilot.

Before entering the space program in 1963, Anders flew all-weather interceptor planes and earned a master's degree in nuclear engineering at the Air Force Institute of Technology. He served a tour of duty at the Air Force Weapons Laboratory at Kirtland Air Force Base, New Mexico.

Astronaut Anders has specialized in the lunar landing vehicle and he is an expert on radiation. As Apollo 8's systems engineer, he monitored the spacecraft's supply of oxygen, power and other consumables. He was also in charge of photography during the mission.

Neil A. Armstrong—The first man to walk on the moon, Astronaut Neil A. Armstrong, was born in Wapakoneta, Ohio, on August 5, 1930. He attended Purdue University, graduating with a bachelor of science degree in aeronautical engineering.

Armstrong was a licensed pilot at 16. Between 1949 and 1952 he was a naval aviator, flying 78 combat missions in Korea.

The future astronaut became a civilian test pilot in 1955. As an aeronautical research pilot at NASA's High Speed Flight Station at Edwards Air Force Base, California, he flew the X-1 rocket plane and several types of jet airplanes. Armstrong was an X-15 project pilot and flew that experimental rocket plane to over 200,000 feet and as fast as 4,000 miles an hour.

Armstrong joined the astronaut program in 1962. He was the command pilot of the Gemini 8 mission that performed the first docking in space and the commander of the history-making Apollo 11 moon-landing mission.

Alan L. Bean—Selected as an astronaut in 1963, Alan L. Bean waited six years for his first space flight. During that time he twice served as a backup crewman.

Bean was born in Wheeler, Texas, on March 15, 1932. As a child he loved airplanes and his ambition was to become a pilot. At the University of Texas, which he attended on a Navy scholarship, he majored in aeronautical engineering. After graduation, Bean became a Navy pilot. He attended the Navy Test Pilot School at Patuxent River, Maryland, and served as a test pilot before he joined the space program.

The slender, self-possessed astronaut was Apollo 12's lunar module pilot and the fourth man to walk on the moon.

Frank Borman—Apollo 8's commander, Astronaut Frank Borman, was born in Gary, Indiana, on March 14, 1928. He entered the Air Force upon graduation from West Point and became a fighter pilot, a career that was interrupted temporarily in 1951 when he ruptured an eardrum during a dive in a jet plane. After x-ray treatments cured the condition, he resumed flying. In 1957, Borman, who has a master of science degree in aeronautical engineering, returned to West Point as an instructor in thermodynamics and fluid mechanics.

Frank Borman was one of nine men selected for NASA's second group of astronauts in 1962. He served as the command pilot of the 330-hour Gemini 7 mission in 1965.

Following his Apollo 8 mission, Borman withdrew from flight duty to become the Manned Spacecraft Center's deputy director of flight-crew operations.

Eugene A. Cernan—Astronaut Eugene A. Cernan was born in Chicago, Illinois, on March 14, 1934. He earned a bachelor of science degree in electrical engineering at Purdue University and became a naval aviator upon graduation. He subsequently received a master of science degree in aeronautical engineering from the United States Naval Postgraduate School.

Cernan joined the astronaut program in 1963. During the Gemini 9 mission, in which he served as pilot, he spent almost two hours outside the spacecraft. He was Apollo 10's lunar module pilot.

Michael Collins—Michael Collins was born on October 31, 1930, in Rome, Italy, where his father was serving as military attaché. After graduating from West Point, the future astronaut joined the Air Force and became a test pilot specializing in jet fighters.

Collins joined the astronaut program in 1963. In 1966 he served as pilot of the Gemini 10 mission during which he completed two periods of extra-vehicular activity. He was Apollo 11's command module pilot.

After the Apollo 11 flight, Collins resigned from NASA's manned space flight program to join the State Department as Assistant Secretary for Public Affairs.

Charles Conrad, Jr.—Apollo 12's commander and third man to set foot on the moon, Charles Conrad, Jr., is a veteran spaceman. Prior to his Apollo 12 flight, he was the pilot of the eight-day Gemini 5 mission in 1965, and the following year he commanded the three-day Gemini 11 mission.

Conrad, whose friends call him "Pete," was born in Philadelphia, Pennsylvania, on June 2, 1930. He graduated from Princeton University with a degree in aeronautical engineering.

The future astronaut, who learned to fly when he was 14, joined the Navy and became a naval aviator. He attended the Navy Test Pilot School at Patuxent River, Maryland. Before transferring to the astronaut program in 1962, he served as a Navy test pilot, flight instructor, performance engineer, and flight safety officer.

Walter Cunningham—Walter Cunningham, Apollo 7's systems engineer, was a research scientist for the Rand Corporation when he became an astronaut in 1963. Cunningham was born in Creston, Iowa, on March 16, 1932. He attended the University of California at Los Angeles where he earned a bachelor's and a master's degree in physics.

Cunningham, who has piloted both conventional and jet aircraft, learned to fly when he joined the Navy in 1951. Later he flew as a Marine reservist.

As a Project Apollo astronaut, Cunningham monitored the design of the spacecraft's electrical and automatic systems, and he helped plan Apollo's lunar surface experiments.

Donn F. Eisele—Astronaut Donn F. Eisele was born in Columbus, Ohio, on June 23, 1930. He graduated from the U.S. Naval Academy in 1952 with a bachelor of science degree. After graduation, the future astronaut chose to serve in the Air Force.

Eisele was awarded a master of science degree in astronautics by the Air Force Institute of Technology and he also graduated from the Air Force Aerospace Research Pilot School at Edwards Air Force Base, California. Before becoming an astronaut in 1963, he was a project engineer and experimental test pilot at the Air Force Special Weapons Center at Kirtland Air Force Base, New Mexico.

In addition to serving as Apollo 7's command module pilot, Astronaut Eisele has participated in the development of the Apollo command, service, and lunar landing modules.

Richard F. Gordon, Jr.—Apollo 12's command module pilot, Richard F. Gordon, Jr., was born in Seattle, Washington, on October 5, 1929. He attended the University of Washington where he joined the Naval Reserve.

After graduation Gordon became a naval aviation cadet. The fledgling pilot soon gave up his long-standing plan to become a dentist. About his first flight he said: "Once I experienced it, I decided that was the only thing I ever wanted to do."

A graduate of the Navy Test Pilot School at Patuxent River, Maryland, Gordon has tested several of the Navy's fast jet fighter planes. In 1961 he won the Bendix Trophy race, flying from Los Angeles to New York in 2 hours and 47 minutes.

Gordon joined the astronaut program in 1963. Prior to his Apollo 12 flight, he served as Gemini 11's pilot and space walker. His commander during that mission was Charles Conrad, who also commanded Apollo 12.

James A. Lovell, Jr.—James A. Lovell, Jr. was born in Cleveland, Ohio, on March 25, 1928. He graduated from the U.S. Naval Academy and from naval pilot training. His military assignments include three years as a test pilot.

After his selection as an astronaut in 1962, Lovell was assigned to Project Gemini. He flew both the Gemini 7 and Gemini 12 missions, and accumulated a record number of days in space. The Apollo 8 flight, for which he was the navigator, added another eight days to the 18 Astronaut Lovell had already spent in space flight.

James A. McDivitt—Apollo 9's commander, James A. McDivitt, was born on June 10, 1929, in Chicago, Illinois. He graduated first in his class from the University of Michigan with a bachelor of science degree in aeronautical engineering.

McDivitt joined the Air Force in 1951 and flew 145 combat missions during the Korean War. He was a test pilot when NASA selected him as an astronaut in 1962.

In 1965 McDivitt commanded the Gemini 4 mission, the first United States space flight that included extravehicular activity.

Following his Apollo 9 mission, McDivitt resigned as an active astronaut although he remained with NASA as a planner of moon landing missions. He later became manager of the Apollo spacecraft program.

Walter M. Schirra, Jr.—Walter M. Schirra, Jr., who was born in Hackensack, New Jersey, on March 12, 1923, took over the controls of an airplane for the first time when he was 13 and soloed at 16. He became a naval aviator after graduation from the U.S. Naval Academy. Schirra flew 90 combat missions during the Korean War and eventually became a Navy test pilot.

Astronaut Schirra made his first space flight in 1962 when he flew a six-orbit mission in Project Mercury's Sigma 7. In 1965 he was the command pilot of the Gemini 6 flight that accomplished the first rendezvous with another manned spacecraft. In 1968 he commanded Apollo 7, the first manned Apollo mission.

After the Apollo 7 flight, Schirra announced his retirement from the astronaut program to enter private business. The veteran spaceman felt that he was getting too old to make another space flight.

Russell L. Schweickart—Russell L. Schweickart was born in Neptune, New Jersey, on October 25, 1935. He attended the Massachusetts Institute of Technology where he earned a bachelor of science degree in aeronautical engineering and a master of science degree in aeronautics and astronautics.

Between 1956 and 1963 Schweickart served as a pilot in the Air Force and the Air National Guard. In 1963 he joined the astronaut program as a civilian. He was lunar module pilot when the LM was tested in space for the first time during the Apollo 9 flight.

David R. Scott—Apollo 9's command module pilot, David R. Scott, was born in San Antonio, Texas, on June 6, 1932. He holds a bachelor of science degree from West Point and a master of science degree in aeronautics and astronautics from the Massachusetts Institute of Technology. His thesis subject was interplanetary navigation.

Scott became an Air Force pilot when he graduated from West Point. He was a test pilot when he joined the astronaut program in 1963. In 1966 he was the pilot of the Gemini 8 mission.

Thomas P. Stafford—Astronaut Thomas P. Stafford was born in Weatherford, Oklahoma, on September 17, 1930. He attended the U.S. Naval Academy and joined the Air Force upon graduation.

As an Air Force officer, Stafford became one of the nation's most experienced test pilots. He is the author of two books on the subject.

Stafford joined the astronaut program in 1962. He served as the pilot of the Gemini 6 mission and the command pilot of Gemini 9. During the Apollo 10 mission, which he commanded, he flew the lunar module, Snoopy, to within 9.4 miles of the moon's surface.

John W. Young—Apollo 10's command module pilot, John W. Young, was born in San Francisco, California, on September 24, 1930. He attended the Georgia Institute of Technology and graduated with a bachelor of science degree in aeronautical engineering.

After graduation from college, Young became a naval aviator. He was a test pilot when he joined the astronaut program in 1962.

Astronaut Young was the pilot of Gemini 3, the first manned Gemini flight, and the command pilot of Gemini 10. He is an expert in orbital rendezvous.

Index

About the Author

When astronauts Armstrong, Aldrin, and Collins returned from their historic trip to the moon, Gene Gurney was an eyewitness of their splashdown in the Pacific and their recovery by the aircraft carrier *Hornet*. He was in charge of the White House Press Center during President Nixon's visit with the Apollo 11 astronauts.

A lieutenant colonel in the U.S. Air Force, Gene Gurney has been a military pilot for 26 years and a command pilot for 10 years. During World War II, Colonel Gurney flew P-40 and P-38 fighters and B-24 and B-17 bombers. After the war he was an Air Force Counter-Intelligence Corps Special Agent investigating espionage, sabotage, and gold smuggling in the Near East and Europe. He has served in Vietnam and has received the Vietnamese Service Medal and the Bronze Star. His present position is Staff Information Officer for the Air Forces in the Pacific.

Gene Gurney is the author of more than 20 books, including two very popular Landmark Books about the earlier U.S. manned-space programs: *Americans Into Orbit* and *Walk in Space*.